Keeping Your Money

KEEPING YOUR MONEY

Real Advice on Wise Investing

Dean McGowan

BROWN BOOKS
PUBLISHING GROUP

Keeping Your Money
Real Advice on Wise Investing

Brown Books Publishing Group
Dallas, TX / New York, NY
www.BrownBooks.com
(972) 381-0009

A New Era in Publishing®

Publisher's Cataloging-In-Publication Data

Names: McGowan, Dean, author.
Title: Keeping your money : real advice on wise investing / Dean McGowan.
Description: Dallas, TX ; New York, NY : Brown Books Publishing Group,
    [2025] | Includes bibliographical references and index.
Identifiers: ISBN: 978-1-61254-714-5 (print) | 978-1-61254-720-6 (ebook) |
    LCCN: 2024949078
Subjects: LCSH: Investments. | Finance, Personal. | Wealth. | BISAC:
    BUSINESS & ECONOMICS / Personal Finance / Investing. |
    BUSINESS & ECONOMICS / Personal Finance / Money Management.
Classification: LCC: HG4521 .M34 2025 | DDC: 332.6--dc23

ISBN 978-1-61254-714-5
EISBN 978-1-61254-720-6
LCCN 2024949078

Printed in Canada
10 9 8 7 6 5 4 3 2 1

For more information or to contact the author, please go to
www.DeanMcGowanAuthor.com.

Table of Contents

Foreword

Some of my best inspiration in life has come from the biographies of extraordinary leaders. I am fortunate in that I grew up with a father who is a truly determined dynamo. Before you dive into the most powerful lessons from his sixty years of investing, you deserve an introduction to Dean McGowan—one of Dallas's most respected advisors and founder of the North Dallas operations of PaineWebber, now UBS Financial Services, the largest assets manager in the world. The original introduction to this book was simply a list of Dean McGowan's achievements over his fifty-five years in the investment advisory business. But at the urging of his family and former UBS associates, my father agreed to include a more detailed account of his personal story, which we hope will explain the origin of the valuable insights in this book—and make for entertaining reading.

—**Spencer McGowan**, Dean McGowan's son, runs the investment advisory firm McGowan Group Asset Management. His radio show, *NetWorth Radio*, airs in Dallas on Saturdays and Sundays.

Introduction

Speaking from Experience

I've been blessed with an extraordinary life. Coming from humble roots in East Texas, where I was born in a shack in the woods without plumbing or electricity, I grew up to become an investment advisor at the largest assets manager in the world. My specialty as a financial advisor? Helping my clients keep their money—by avoiding all the common mistakes that make this so incredibly difficult for most people.

All of this is to say I haven't always been financially successful. My journey to becoming a seasoned financial advisor took many twists and turns, and I want to share some of the high points—and hopefully the humor—of my hardscrabble upbringing that made me the man I am today.

I was born in 1938 in a small frame house with no plumbing or electricity, on a dirt road in East Texas near the small town of Timpson. My father, Youree McGowan, who had only a third-grade education, had lost a farm during the Depression, which was still going on when I was born. My father worked for many years as a sharecropper, and later he managed a local farm and ranch. I was seven years old when the Rural Electrification Association built electric lines in the neighborhood and my dad wired the house and put in plumbing.

Then, when I was eleven, my family moved closer to town, and I started working in the local drug store.

Those were hard times, and even kids were expected to contribute financially. I got a work permit from school and worked afternoons, evenings, and weekends. In fact, I worked two jobs—something that became a pattern in my life. My next job as a teenager was working as a clerk at the local Taylor's Hardware Store. While working there, I noticed that the store shelves were leaning, faded and unlevel, and so I took the initiative to replace them, rebuilding all the counters in the store and overhauling the office area. A second job came with the East Texas tomato season, as farmers needed someone to unload and pack crates into rail cars for shipping. The interview for that position was the most bizarre in my life—they told me I had to get past the burly door guard to earn the job, and the ensuing fight was a bloody proof of determination. It took all my Judo skills to get that job!

With my earnings, I was able to buy all of my own school supplies and most of my clothes.

Even with two jobs, I wasn't going to miss out on extracurricular activities. I wrote for the high school paper, played in the school band, and qualified for the tristate band as well as regional competitions in speaking, number sense, slide rule, and typing. I had the honor to be elected class president for three years.

After graduation I got into the University of Texas at Austin, but there was a problem: I had to enter UT on probation, make up course deficiencies (several required courses were not taught in my small high school), and make my grades—all in the first semester.

I could pay for college since I had worked and saved so much during high school. I was dropped off at the University of Texas in Austin with a suitcase, two cardboard boxes, and $451 in my bank account.

I didn't have a car until after college, so I would hitchhike home from Austin to East Texas, 265 miles through the Davy Crockett Forest, every Thanksgiving, Christmas, and Easter. Hitchhiking was popular in those days, and students would often put college stickers on their bags for identification.

During college I lived in a co-op—these were popular on many campuses in the last century. The residents ran their own house, doing the cleaning, much of the cooking, the maintenance, and the financial management. At different times I served as maintainer, treasurer, and president of the co-op, and also as chairman of the Co-Op Presidents' Council and on the Dean of Men's Advisory Council.

Summer jobs in college were a true adventure. For two summers I worked on a construction site in Houston, and I was assigned to the downtown skyscrapers, walking the beams and delivering tools and materials to the iron workers and welders. Lunch was out of a lunch kit up on the beams because there was no way down for the lunch break. There were no tethers, nets, or safety straps in those days. There was no OSHA.

As if working on the high-rises wasn't thrilling enough, I also drove ambulances at night and on the weekends so that I had a place to sleep at the hospital. The ambulance was a great fit for a guy like me—I have been a fast driver my whole life. One night, I was even a little *too* fast, and I arrived at a gun fight before the police got there. I had to hide behind the ambulance until the police showed up!

My first brush with finance came when I worked in the pharmacy at age eleven. At the time my dad had asked me to check with the various businesses who had extended him credit during the depths of the Depression—grocery stores, hardware stores, and the like. There were no unpaid bills. My takeaway from that effort was that it's essential to always do the paperwork.

After graduation, I went to work in business. I was privileged to become the youngest partner of the regional investment firm Schneider, Burnet, and Hickman. Eventually I served terms as mutual funds manager and pension funds manager of the firm, in addition to my investment advisory business. Later, at PaineWebber, I was assistant branch manager and then branch manager and vice president of the firm. At UBS, the succeeding firm, I served as branch manager, vice president, and senior vice president.

During my term as branch manager at UBS, the Series 7 exam, the primary securities-licensing test for financial advisors, became seriously out of date. This exam is often the first requirement for continued employment as a financial advisor; failing can result in immediate termination. I was asked to serve on the New York Stock Exchange (NYSE) Education Committee with the objective of rewriting the entire battery of three thousand questions. From 1981 to 1984, I served on that NYSE committee, which rewrote the test. (My son, Spencer, endured the stressful requirements to pass this very exam in 1986 and scored a 90 out of 100.)

A key principle that has shaped my career and life is that we are all meant to serve others. I believe my job is to serve.

For that reason, it has been important for me to take on service opportunities alongside my work as an assets manager. So I have served on the School of Management Advisory Board as well as the Finance Department and Investment Boards at the University of Texas at Dallas, and I act as a mentor to MBA students at the university. I have also been privileged to serve in leadership roles at the Community Christian Church in Richardson, Texas, and later to teach Sunday School and serve as a coach to minority families as a part of Project Hope at the Christ United Methodist Church in Plano.

Throughout my life I have always believed that exercise and physical activity are necessary for an excellent quality of life. In college I was sports manager for the University Christian Church, played on various intramural teams, competed on the university judo team, and in 1959 was the runner-up wrestling champion of the University of Texas. As a "senior citizen," I have been privileged to play six Texas state championship games, and even one national championship. I skied until I was eighty, and today—in my eighties—I still play tennis!

Another thing I do, even in retirement, is score my performance daily on a scale ranging from criminally negligent, to slacker, to celebrating the high goal achieved for the day.

As a professional financial advisor, my sacred mission has been to serve others. I made it my rule to never refuse help to anyone, whether it was likely to result in an account or not.

If your objective is to get rich quick through risky stock trading, this book is not for you. My objective is to offer coaching on *how to keep your money*. Growing up the way I did, I understand the value of money, and I am keenly aware of how hard it is to accumulate—and to keep. My first priority has always been to preserve my clients' money—not necessarily to make them rich.

Over the course of this book, we will cover many common ways in which people turn good money into serious losses. It is my endeavor that you proceed to the final chapter and take seriously the simple procedures that will look after your hard-earned money and keep it working for you later in life, and maybe even for your heirs.

The money (or lack thereof) that you will have in the future depends heavily on how you deal with saving and accumulating your assets. The process is simple, but the discipline is rigorous. The correct approach involves avoiding many temptations.

Hopefully some of the stories here will have an impact on your future actions and help you resist the many bad decisions that can all too easily gobble up your wealth. It's not rocket science; it's the simple discipline to avoid careless mistakes, tend to your accumulated assets, and opt for income and quality in your investments. Reading this book should not be a task. It should be entertaining, informative, relevant, and easily understood. I hope you find it that way.

Primer for Chapters 1–4

Learning Not to Be Stupid

If we intend to polish our investing behaviors, we can start by learning what constitutes bad behavior. As children, a loud "no" often accompanies any behavior deemed wrong or inappropriate by our parents. Avoiding many of those actions later becomes obvious to us, but we had to go through the learning process first.

Many of the bad investment practices I cover in this book will be apparent while others might seem a bit new, yet becoming keenly aware of bad behaviors and then avoiding them is a learning process. The early chapters of this book deal with examples of bad investment practices that can torpedo our hard-earned money.

Once we learn what "no" really means in our investing process, we can then proceed with good discipline.

Chapter 1

Stupid Things People Do with Their Money

I t is only now that I am a bit removed from the financial profession that I can ask the following question:

Why do people pay financial advisors in the first place?

A major motivation for getting professional financial advice is the hope of making more money. Now, I have already warned you that if your objective is to get rich quick, this book is not for you. Get-rich-quick is a promise that sells a lot of financial advice. But here's a secret that experienced financial advisors know: the real trick to being financially comfortable isn't acquiring more money but holding on to the money you already have. While this may seem simple enough, it's a lot harder than it looks. And that is exactly where this book comes in—to coach you on how to *keep* your money.

Everyone who works in the investment business for any period of time has observed some very illogical decisions made by an investor and has wanted to grab that person by the shoulders and say, "Get real." There are many strategies to hold on to your assets, and I will get to these later on. But even more important are the ways that people most often *lose* their money. Here, to begin with, is a preview of some of the stupid things that financial advice professionals have seen on a regular basis:

Selling at the Lows

It has always been a mystery to me that I can be run over by a frantic shopper in Dillard's, Nordstrom's, or Macy's during a triple-throw-down sale by someone who would not even consider a blue-chip stock when it has declined by 30 percent. And those same people are the ones who will sell those stocks when they are way down and often very, very cheap.

There have always been bear markets, and there always will be bear markets. A black swan is always lurking, and the best of the professionals do not know when the next one will appear. So it is extremely important that an investor holds onto good securities through the bear markets. We never know when the next down market will be, and we don't know when the rebound will occur. What we do know is that the rebound will come in huge percentage moves, and we need to be ready for it.

In a Fidelity Investments study (which we will examine further in chapter 10), missing just the ten best days of the stock market over a forty-year period cost one investor more than half of the net returns.[1] What this demonstrates is that while we never know when the big declines are coming, we *really* don't know when the bottoms will occur. Missing these initial rebounds can be extremely costly.

Buying at the Highs

The fear of missing out on a rising market will entice people to throw money in at high prices—often the same people who would never consider buying when stocks are cheap. Then those same investors will measure their performance from those high points and never calculate the performance from the low valuation points. This is important because, as we will see later, missing just the ten best days in a forty-year period can remove over half of your stock returns—and over one-fourth of all the best days occur less than ninety days after a bear market bottom. I prefer to buy all my clothes at the department store when they have a triple-throwdown sale, and I prefer to buy my stocks at the low points instead of the high points in the stock market.

Take, for example, an investor who bought the Dow Jones index on October 19, 1987—the day of the largest stock market dip at 22 percent. By the end of the year, the market's recovery would take it back up over 11 percent, while an investor who bought the same index at the year's high would finish the year down over 28 percent. Yet the investor looking only at year-end prices would say that 1987 was a year of no change, as the stock market ended up relatively even, with just a 0.6 percent increase.

Investing in Illiquid Investments

An illiquid investment is anything you put your money into that can't be quickly and easily turned into cash without a substantial loss. We will cover this more in chapter 6 of this book, but it is important to consider your potential gains *and losses* whenever you are considering a new investment opportunity, no matter how fruitful it may seem. An investor who would never put more than $10,000 in a single stock will often invest $50,000 or more in a private venture offered by some "friend of a friend."

Overinvesting in One Asset

Even if an investor maintains liquidity, an investor managing their own portfolio must avoid the temptation to overinvest in just a few assets. The professionals in the business know that any stock, no matter the promoted quality, can be down 50 percent or more in any given year. If an investor is heavily invested in such a stock, the performance of their portfolio that year will be ruined. Chapter 4 of this book will go into more detail on this mistake—and how not to make it.

Buying on Margin

Using borrowed money to buy investments can destroy several years of good returns. An account with 50 percent borrowed money will decline by 50 percent in equity with just a 25 percent decline in prices. For example, a $50,000 account with another $50,000 borrowed on margin experiencing a 25 percent decline will lose $25,000. That's half the initial equity! With only the remaining $25,000 in equity, the investor will be forced to sell when the margin call comes. Under the Federal Reserve regulation on margin, or Reg T, a margin call is required when the equity in stock accounts reaches 25 percent. Most firms that offer margin accounts have higher house rules and will issue margin calls when the equity level declines to 30 percent, at which point the investor will face a margin call and be forced to sell if unable to provide more money to the account. That level would leave the investor with only $15,000 equity against a $50,000 debit, plus an interest that is normally charged monthly on margin accounts. In fact, many margin calls have been issued once an interest charge is made on the account. Let's look at these numbers side by side:

Price Status	Borrowed $	Investment Value
100%	$50,000	$100,000
25% Decline	$50,000	$25,000
30% Decline	$50,000	$15,000

At this point, the investor gets a margin call and is still paying interest on the borrowed $50,000.

Acting on a Non-Investor's Advice

Whether your assets came through your own hard work or an inheritance, you owe it to yourself and your family to diligently protect those assets. Acting on the advice of someone with no successful record as an investor can be dangerous. In chapter 9 of this book we will address selecting a financial advisor, but the most important thing to remember is that someone giving financial advice should have a proven financial background and access to financial resources, including research.

Speculation

The tendency to speculate in the hope of making quick money can overwhelm all reason. "Speculation" covers a wide range of topics, and also includes a lot of dangers. Some of these are options, credit default swaps and other derivatives, penny stocks, commodities, and new technologies. Chapter 4 of this book will cover speculations such as these in more depth, but for now, it is enough to recognize that the investor in any of the so-called "investments" below is taking an undue risk by not engaging in long-term investments.

Gambling

Gambling is a touchy subject for many folks. People who clip coupons and watch prices at the grocery store and restaurants will spend hundreds or even thousands of dollars gambling, and then try to explain to themselves and others why they made such stupid decisions.

Addiction to gambling is just like any other addiction: It can ruin a fortune. It can ruin a family. And it can ruin one's perspective on life. Just like with narcotics and alcohol, an addict is always in danger of slipping back into the habit.

Chapter 3 of this book illustrates some of the massive gambling losses made by some successful entertainers and athletes. The poker tables, crap tables, slot machines, and lottery tickets can be addictive, but they can often have disastrous outcomes.

Falling for Scams

In today's world of robocalls, foreign solicitations, data hacking, and internet phishing schemes, the risks of being sucked into a false situation are high. Seniors are especially vulnerable to these risks. For example, the *Dr. Phil Show* recently featured a segment on a lady giving her entire savings of $300,000 to a supposed contractor in need of money. This "contractor" was later exposed as a guy in Nigeria having romantic conversations with this lady and other women—and extracting money for nonexistent opportunities.

Spending All That You Earn

There will always be unexpected emergencies in everyone's life. But to spend your emergency savings fund and not replace those savings is to invite disaster. There is always a myriad of reasons why you need to overspend, but the reality is that you can only build wealth by spending less than you earn. Many of us who have attended college or spent time in the military know that you can exist quite well living in very small quarters, eating inexpensive food, wearing unexciting clothes, and working hard.

Overspending is particularly tempting when you are building a family. You need transportation. You need medical attention. You need food for the family. And you expect your income to increase as you progress in your job. It is really important, however, to distinguish between needs and wants. You must address the things you really need and see if you can finance those purchases, and you have to evaluate the things you want and make sure you're not confusing those desires with true needs.

Lastly, it is vital to *never underestimate your spending requirements.* Buying a big house or an expensive car without planning for the costs of maintenance is letting the drive to spend—which is often the drive to belong—override rational thinking and prudence. Not ignoring spending requirements is crucial to living within one's income.

Chapter 2

Savings Practices

Over my many years in the investment advisory business, I've noticed that the profiles of investors don't change; there are savers, and there are spenders. There is a wide gulf between the two tendencies, with few in between.

It was Thomas Jefferson who said, "Never spend your money before you have it."

Don't Spend Your Principal

It's shocking to see how many people who suddenly come into large sums of money will quickly spend that money instead of investing it. A normal investment return on a $100,000 principal will give the owner around $7,000 per year in net returns—spending that principal money will reduce the owner's income by $7,000 for every remaining year of that person's life. If we're talking about $1,000,000, the return level becomes around $70,000 per year. At $70,000 per year, that person should never be stressed for money.

In the advisory business, we can usually tell within the first fifteen minutes of talking with an heir whether that person will have the money five years from receiving the settlement. If an heir begins the conversation with the need for a new car, a bigger house, and the desire to see Europe, the odds of that person keeping their inheritance drop significantly. It is at this point in the conversation that some reason must be injected into the discussion. The more the heir dwells on material goods or experiences, the more likely that spending will dominate their actions—and fritter away their inheritance.

We see this scene played out not only with inheritances but also with bonuses, entertainment contracts, lottery winnings, and major sports contracts. All forms of sudden income are subject to the evaluation of needs versus wants. For example, I might say that I need a new car. But today's vehicles are designed to run for hundreds of thousands of miles with reasonable maintenance. My "need" for a new car might be because my neighbor has one, or because my stature with friends and business acquaintances improves if my car appears to be new and pretty.

We are likely to be better savers and investors if we live in smaller houses, drive our cars longer, and buy fewer things than our peers. Our temptation to buy things can wreck our saving and investing plans—every dollar of principal you spend will reduce your income for the rest of your life.

Avoid Forced Selling

A margin call can force the sale of an account—usually at the worst of times, when the market is down. The lack of savings to cover an emergency or borrowing irresponsibly can also force a sale at an undesirable time, and the recognition that some investment has turned out badly can force liquidation of a private venture or other project.

The takeaway? Don't buy on margin. Save for emergencies. Invest prudently. And never borrow irresponsibly.

Save for Emergencies

It can be really boring to talk about savings. But everyone must address the subject or be caught without funds when emergencies occur. What I'm talking about here is an emergency funds account for unexpected expenses. This looks different for everyone, but your calculation should include enough to cover unexpected auto and home repairs or uninsured medical expenses. The larger your savings account, the more appropriate higher deductibles will be on your insurance policies—and the lower your insurance premiums.

The emergency savings account should not be considered part of your long-term investment fund. You should save for emergencies, and you should invest for the long term. It is only once you have accumulated an adequate emergency savings account that the investment process can begin. At that point, every dollar put into the investment pot should increase your future standard of living.

Don't Overpay Uncle Sam

Tax laws are changing constantly. The best advice I can offer is to use logical tax advantages whenever possible. The key term here is "logical," because there can be a lot of variations. A good CPA can be very helpful.

Let's look at just one example. An investor putting money into a tax-free IRA or 401(k) could put $1,000 into the account and compound the returns tax free for thirty years. The $1,000 would grow to $8,755 using an average equity-investor return of 7.5 percent. If that investor has a tax rate of 25 percent, that same amount invested privately would be worth only around $5,164. Also, if we consider that that money is subject to taxes before its investment, then we must deduct 25 percent, which cuts the investor's thirty-year return to $3,873, less than half of the tax-free investment. It is true that the investor must pay taxes when the withdrawal occurs, but the key here is *when*. In this case, if we assume a 100 percent withdrawal after the thirty years, we will have $566 versus the $873—a 70 percent better return. A tax-free accumulation will always outperform a taxed rate of return, even in an environment of rising taxes.

So using IRA and 401(k) accounts can improve the long-term return on your investments because the deposits are made *before* taxes. In many cases, these returns are 25 percent or more than if you had invested the money after taxes, and the returns accumulate for years without being taxed. All 401(k) accounts are eligible to be rolled over to an IRA when you change jobs or retire, and this is totally tax free unless the owner has reached the required withdrawal age, which is currently seventy-three. Only about 4 percent of the total needs to be withdrawn (and taxed) annually when the withdrawal age is reached. The required minimum withdrawal is based on average life expectancy, and it increases slightly each year.

Roth IRA deposits, on the other hand, are made after taxes. The first necessary condition for a Roth is that you do not expect to need the money for a long, long time. To avoid tax penalties, the money must remain on deposit for at least five years, regardless of the investor's age. But once deposited, the money enjoys a huge advantage. The returns on a Roth IRA can accumulate tax free for the entire life of the owner, and no withdrawals are required. Many people who change jobs and are in good financial health will opt to roll over their 401(k) deposits to a Roth and let the net funds grow tax free for decades (note that taxes must be paid on the funds at the time of the rollover). There have been many proposals in Washington to kill the Roth IRA, and investors should be alert to future legal possibilities at the time of investing.

If you have exhausted tax-free options in investing, or if you wish to maintain some access to the invested funds, then you should look at opening investment accounts in your personal name. To do so safely and prudently, you must ensure that any cash is within the FDIC-insured limits, any investments are made through investment firms whose assets are housed at the Depository Trust Company (DTC), and all accounts are in the investor's name; no money should go to accounts under a third party's name.

The Early Bird Gets the Worm

You might have heard the advice to start early when it comes to investing, and this is true. Investing early is important primarily because of compound interest. Look closely at the chart below: The first investor starts at age eighteen with $1,000 per year and contributes only until age twenty-five. The second investor begins at age twenty-five with $1,000 per year and continues with that same investment rate until the age of sixty. At a 10 percent return rate, the long-term stock-market average, the second investor never catches up with the first investor.

Compare the two scenarios: Investor 1 contributes $1,000 to his investment account annually from the age of eighteen to twenty-five, and then stops contributing. Investor 2 contributes $1,000 to his investment account annually from the age of twenty-five to sixty. Investor 1 began seven years earlier, but Investor 2 never stopped contributing to his account.

The first chart below shows the account balance of each investor over the forty-two-year investment period. For simplicity, the calculations assume a 10 percent annual return on investment, which is the historical average for the S&P 500 index. Note that Investor 2 never catches up with Investor 1 despite continuing the $1,000 annual contributions until age sixty.

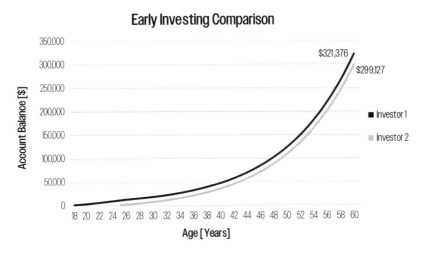

The next two charts distinguish investment from savings gains over the forty-two-year period.

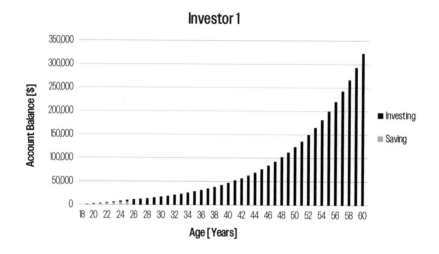

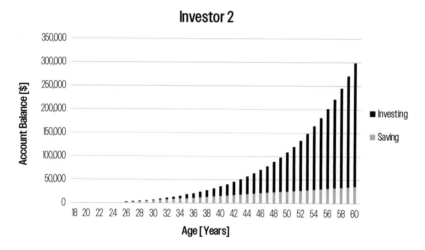

The main factor that contributes to the gap between the investors' results is the seven-year head start of Investor 1. Notice that those seven years make a particular difference in the latter years, when the account balances, and consequently the interest earnings, are large. Most importantly, by investing $8,000 cumulatively for the first eight years, Investor 1 grew his money to over $321,000!

The primary lesson here is that investing early is very important. The reality, though, is that most people are not able to invest much in the early stages of their lives. But you have to start somewhere, and the best time is as soon as you pay off any high-interest debts and have something in the emergency savings account.

Follow Charlie Munger's Advice

Charlie Munger was a senior VP with Berkshire Hathaway, and the trusted partner of Warren Buffet. His advice on savings is: "The first $100,000 is a bitch but you gotta do it. I don't care what you have to do—if it means walking everywhere and not eating anything that wasn't purchased with a coupon, find a way to get your hands on $100,000. After that, you can ease off the gas a little bit."

As inflation deflates the dollar and the numbers increase, the principle remains the same. You have to get those first dollars to invest. While chapter 7 addresses the resources available to you as the level of your investments rises to $250,000, then $500,000 and $1,000,000, in the early years, the task is to get your investments started and build upon those numbers.

Earn Dividends

Stock incomes, or dividends, have ranged from one-third to 40 percent of the total average long-term stock return. According to one often-repeated slogan, "the only reason to own a stock is its ultimate ability to pay me an income." CEOs and corporate boards are under constant pressure to pay out a reasonable amount of the company profit in dividends, and the rate of increase for dividends has been around 4 percent annually for stocks in the major indexes. Although dividend income will vary with the economic cycle, the income stream from good portfolios has been relatively constant. At the time of this book, General Mills has paid dividends for 116 years and has *never* reduced its dividend.

Take Advantage of Dollar-Cost Averaging

Dollar-cost averaging is a strategy important for all investors—both new and experienced—to understand. This strategy helps protect investors from market volatility by investing the same amount of money in a specific stock at regular intervals, regardless of price. Below is an example of the strategy in action. This example shows extreme fluctuation in an investment, but it illustrates the nature of dollar-cost averaging and will help you understand how the process works.

If you save and invest $1,000 per month during a period of extreme price fluctuations, you can see the results in simple terms. The price of this investment starts at $10 per share, goes to $5 per share, and then returns to $10. It is assumed that you are buying a diversified mutual fund or exchange-traded fund (ETF), where fractional shares are available.

Month 1: $1,000 invested at $10 per share = 100 shares
Month 2: $ 1,000 invested at $9 per share = 111.1 shares
Month 3: $1,000 invested at $8 per share = 125 shares
Month 4: $1,000 invested at $7 per share = 142.86 shares
Month 5: $1,000 invested at $6 per share = 166.67 shares
Month 6: $1,000 invested at $5 per share = 200 shares
Month 7: $1,000 invested at $6 per share = 166.67 shares
Month 8: $1,000 invested at $7 per share = 142.86 shares
Month 9: $1,000 invested at $8 per share = 125 shares
Month 10: $1,000 invested at $9 per share = 111.1 shares
Month 11: $1,000 at $10 per share = 100 shares
Month 12: $1,000 at $10 per share = 100 shares

TOTAL SPENT: $12,000
TOTAL SHARES: 1591.26
AVERAGE COST: $7.54 per share
NET VALUE: $15,912.60
NET PROFIT: 32.5 percent

The virtue of this system is that you buy fewer shares at a higher cost and more shares when the price is lower. That way you get the most shares at the lowest price. As a result, the return is impressive.

Choose Wisely between Funds and Managed Accounts

When starting to invest, one of the many difficult decisions you will face is whether to invest in funds or managed accounts.

Unless you have more than $25,000 (preferably more than $100,000) to invest, the wise decision is to go with funds—either mutual funds or ETFs. There are two reasons for this: Firstly, the commissions are very high on small trades, primarily those less than $5,000. Also, management fees on small accounts, especially those less than $100,000, are very high. Your choices improve once you have $100,000 or $500,000, but you should still be very conscious of expenses. Beginning investors should therefore concentrate on accumulating funds to invest in a managed portfolio once they are beyond this threshold.

Understand the Difference between Weighted and Unweighted Indexes

Understanding the differences between weighted and unweighted indexes can be difficult, but it is vital to making smart investments. Let's consider a real-life example: As I was writing this book, in May of 2024, the S&P 500 index was up for the year by 9.1 percent! However, if you take out the top seven stocks, the Magnificent Seven, the index was down by 0.5 percent—it was a true case of the tail wagging the dog. Seven stocks dominated the performance of the other 493 stocks in the index because they were the very large tech companies like Apple or Microsoft worth over $2 trillion each. The smallest companies in the index were worth around $4 billion each. That means that the top company "weighed" as much as 500 times as much as the smallest company.

The S&P 500 index is a capital-weighted index, meaning that the net capital worth of the company will determine its weight in the index. The Dow Jones index, on the other hand, is price weighted, meaning that the highest-priced stock will carry more weight than the cheapest stock. Most mutual funds do not adhere to the weighted-average practice, although they will allow successfully growing companies to achieve higher weightings in the portfolios. While the mutual funds will vary their position sizes and let their winners grow, they will almost never let a large position get dominant in a portfolio. Large positions in the S&P index, at the time of this writing, are over 70 times the size of smaller ones. Index ETFs are constructed to be identical to the index that it mirrors, and thus by definition must reflect the prices and carry the same weighting as the index in question. Weighting will sometimes significantly distort the performances of weighted indexes in comparison to well-balanced portfolios.

Now we get to the real question: Should your investments be capital-weighted? Probably not. If you want your investments to match the performance of an index, then you should just buy that index ETF and be done with it. But if you want consistent, long-term performance with more limited risk, then you might lean toward a non-weighted portfolio. Yet another consideration you must weigh is that the dividend income is higher in non-weighted portfolios. Most managed accounts are not capital-weighted and, in the long term, will be less affected by the higher volatile swings that weighted portfolios are subject to.

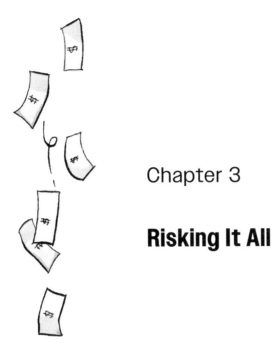

Chapter 3

Risking It All

A large portion of this book could be included under this topic—risking it all. Any time you make an investment that involves the majority of your net worth, you should ask yourself, "Am I risking it all?" In gambling, that's called "betting the farm." While in the early days of our country this phrase quite literally meant betting the farm as the family's primary asset, today you can "bet the farm" by tying up too much money in just one investment. This tends to happen when you overestimate the investment value of an invention, borrow large sums of money, fall for scams, gamble away assets, or overinvest in ventures and private investments.

Gambling

If you play poker, the longevity of your time in the game depends upon the size of your bet, and that time is guaranteed to be short if you bet all your assets on each hand. You may say that would be a stupid thing to do—but it is amazing how often it happens. The odds of failure are immensely high on any one bet, investment, venture, or game.

If you are worth $100,000 and you take $100 to a poker party, that party can be considered nothing more than fun and games. But if you take $20,000 to the party, you are in danger of gambling away your wealth. People who spend time in Las Vegas have seen gamblers calling banks or credit card companies to access funds they had not intended to spend. And anyone with a gambler in their family or circle of friends has heard the sad excuses:

- *"I'll stop when I get even."*
- *"I'm overdue for a big win."*
- *"After this trip, I'm through gambling."*
- *"I can stop any time I want."*

Any expenditure at an amount above the level of entertainment that buys nothing, has no productive value, and has a high risk of no return is a gamble. Gambling does not have to take place at a slot machine or involve a deck of cards—and it can be even more costly when it involves the risky investment of your assets.

Avoiding Bad Investments

When I say bad investment, I don't just mean an investment that loses money. You can acquire a good investment, become impatient when the price drops, sell it at a loss, and lose your money. That's a bad result, but the original purchase was actually a good investment. Bad timing and lack of patience does not mean that high-quality blue-chip stocks or good real estate properties are bad investments. What I want to talk about here is something different. I want to warn you against investments that you should never put your money in.

As we discussed in chapter 2, a saying often quoted in investment circles states that "The only reason to own a stock is its ultimate ability to pay me a dividend." It's not a bad idea for a beginning investor to start with this slogan and apply it to all of their possible investment opportunities. You should ask yourself, "will this investment pay me an income?" Note:

- Gold does not pay a dividend.
- Raw land does not pay a dividend.
- A straight flush does not pay a dividend.
- Most stocks that have never earned money do not pay dividends.
- Most private ventures do not pay an annual income.

Most of the good, sound, and dependable investments that may sound a bit boring *do* pay a dividend. It's really easy to get excited about an opportunity that you hear about through a friend or relative or some other promoter. However, you should always ask the proper questions before investing your assets. Beyond the question of whether this is a high-quality investment that will pay you income, you should ask yourself:

- Am I staying diversified? Or would this investment be too large a portion of my portfolio?
- Am I transferring money out of accounts in my name to someone else's with no guarantee of a return?
- Is this investment liquid?
- What do I know about the management of this enterprise? Is it trustworthy?

Investing is very different from speculating. It is imperative that you constantly watch where your money is invested and concentrate on the important hallmarks of good investing—safety, liquidity, income, and a good long-term outlook.

Common Financial Scams

Scams occur when perpetrators let their greed prevail over ethical behavior—and the victims let greed win over common sense. An uncontrollable desire to get ahead quickly will tempt people to act outside the law or trust criminal scammers, and no amount of education protects us from falling for the various scams that plague our society.

In the fall of 2022, the online consumer news publication *ConsumerAffairs* listed the top ten scams of the year:[1]

1. Identity Theft
2. Imposter Scams
3. Debt Collection Scams
4. Investment Related Scams
5. Business Opportunity Scams
6. Prizes, Lotteries, & Sweepstakes
7. Health Care Scams
8. Advance Payment Scams
9. Foreign Money Offers & Fake Checks
10. Foreclosure Relief & Debt Management

We face potential scams on an almost daily basis, and a vast majority of them fit into one of the above categories. When an unknown person presents you with an opportunity to quickly make money or avoid a serious risk, it's critical that you ask why and by whom the offer is being made. The elderly are most vulnerable to these scams, but everyone is at risk, and we should all be on our guard against these offers.

Variations of these scams are numerous, but we will go over a few of the most common.

Friends and Love Interests

We've all been told to be careful about who we trust on the internet, but the quest to be admired or wanted captivates many people. The more time we spend connecting with people online, the more we are exposed to possible scams by a devious person seeking sex or money. Many of these risks can be avoided by simply ignoring emails or asking a few more questions of the person sending the unsolicited message.

Fake Bills and Invoices

One common scheme is to send out a fake bill and offer to clear it online by credit card. The bill may be for such a small amount that the recipient pays it quickly, without checking, and forgets all about it. Then, at some future date, the recipient is charged a huge amount by the scammer, who is almost always impossible to identify. Extreme care should be used before you pay a bill, however small, that suddenly appears from an unknown source.

Home Improvements

Each state has different rules on how contractors should be registered, and the quality of even licensed contractors will vary widely. Shortly after a tornado or strong windstorm in an area, roofing contractors will appear in great numbers to assist homeowners with assessing and repairing their roof damage—whether they are real or not. Before you know it, your "contractor" has scammed you out of thousands of dollars, and you are still left with the damage to repair.

This problem extends to all forms of home repair, and homeowners should be very careful about researching and vetting any potential contractors. There are many extremely competent home repair companies out there, and we can be happy that these facilities exist. We must, however, be diligent in finding the good ones.

Ponzi Schemes

A Ponzi scheme is a scam in which the money invested by new financial backers is used to pay off earlier investors looking for a payout. It's essentially "robbing Peter to pay Paul," and Charles Ponzi used it so well to defraud investors in the U.S. and Canada that it became known as the Ponzi scheme.

The original Ponzi scheme began in the summer of 1919. Ponzi set up a small office in Boston and began selling investors on his expertise in the exchange of postal-reply coupons and the opportunities that were available in exchange rate differences between the currencies and postal rates of different countries.[2] The idea was complex, and in fact, he never really put the system into operation. He was a master, however, at soliciting investors, and he began to bring in lots of money. When investors started giving him over $1 million per week (over $15 million in today's money), he bought a controlling interest in a small bank and funneled the newly invested money through it. The investors ranged from wealthy people to his own chauffeur, and they included almost two-thirds of the Boston police force. At the height of his scheme Ponzi reportedly had seventeen thousand investors.

Global Investment Scams

Several years ago, I got a call from a client wanting to withdraw half of his IRA account for an "exceptional opportunity." A small joint account he had with his wife and a modest IRA represented all of their savings from many years of hard work. My client said that he could not talk about the opportunity, but that it was exceptional, and he expected to be back with a major deposit once he capitalized on this investment.

I cautioned the client about short-term opportunities, reminded him that the withdrawal would be 100 percent taxable because it was coming from the IRA, and pleaded with him to reassess this opportunity and participate in a more limited way. He told me that the tax liability would be insignificant when compared to the return. Then, just a couple of weeks later, the client came back asking for the balance of the IRA, saying that the return on the funds would be available very soon and would be huge.

I heard nothing from the client for several weeks, until he came back asking if I could refer him to "a good attorney." It turned out that the "great investment opportunity" had been the completion of a secret and nearly finished project for the Nigerian government, and the promised payment was supposed to be "about ten-fold the investment in a very short period of time." In reality, there was no project, no investment opportunity, and certainly no payoff for my client. The investing couple was essentially penniless, they owed the IRS a significant sum, and both were too old to return to the workforce. Much like the woman featured on *Dr. Phil*, they learned to think twice before sending their assets abroad.

Scams through the Ages

It's not just ordinary people who fall for these scams. There are plenty of stories about well-known public figures whose handling of money illustrates the importance of avoiding scams, not getting caught up in the fads and crazes, and simply not spending more than you earn.

Some of the people I profile here were scammers and some of them were victims, but none of them ended up keeping their money. In every real-world example below, whether it is recent celebrity news or centuries-old history, the lesson is the same—don't fall for investments that sound too good to be true, investigate opportunities diligently, don't let greed outweigh your common sense, and keep your eyes on the long-term value of any potential investments.

Bernard L. Madoff

One of the largest scams in history, and a good example of a Ponzi scheme, is the Bernie Madoff scandal. Madoff began his professional career as a stockbroker and started a private investment firm in 1960. In 2001, he changed it from a private investment fund to an LLC, which allowed him to use new investments to pay off old investors. Bernie Madoff was the sole stockholder.

Madoff's firm had all the hallmarks of a behind-the-scenes investment operation—something you should be very cautious about as an investor. It was not a publicly offered mutual fund. It did not house investors' assets at the DTC. It was not a member of the New York Stock Exchange. An investor putting money into Madoff's firm was at the mercy of the success or failure of a non-public corporation.

The operation brought in millions and then billions of dollars. At one point it was reported to be a $65 billion company.[3] And yet the whole time there was little an investor could do to check up on the Madoff investments. Investors were given statements prepared by the firm, and the payouts and returns continued in an orderly manner—until they didn't. It later came out that the accounting firm signing off on those statements was a three-person firm with just one accountant, not the major players you would expect from a company of this size. While Madoff was awaiting sentencing in 2009, he told SEC investigators that he could have been caught as early as 2003 if anyone had bothered to check with the DTC on his claimed securities holdings.[4] Starting in 1992, there had been six formal SEC investigations into the firm because of reported suspicions about the company, but Madoff wasn't exposed and arrested until 2008. The exact losses will never be determined, but the difference between investments and recovered assets was between $12 and $20 billion. That is much less than the reported $65 billion, but still a huge scam, the biggest Ponzi scheme in history. In June of 2009, Mr. Madoff was sentenced to a total of 150 years in prison.

The Tulip Craze

Speaking of history, one of the biggest investment disasters in world history took place in seventeenth-century Holland. In the 1600s, Dutch merchants were at the center of the East Indies trade. Amsterdam merchants would sail out of the Netherlands with goods from Europe, sell them in the East Indies, and bring back goods to be sold at home. The Dutch economy became one of the leading economies of the world, and the country had the highest per capita income in the world.

In the midst of this international trading economy, the so-called "Tulip Mania" swept through Holland. The Dutch went crazy for new varieties of tulips, and tulip bulbs were traded for exorbitant amounts of money. At one point in 1637, tulip bulbs "were being sold for 10 times the annual income of a skilled artisan."[5] The 1841 book *Extraordinary Popular Delusions & the Madness of Crowds* reported on an incident in which twelve acres of land were offered for just one Semper Augusta tulip bulb.[6]

Many theories have been proposed about how this craze got started and escalated to such a ridiculous level, but there is never just one single explanation for an economic bubble and the resulting crash. Compare the tech bubble of 1999 and 2000 and the resulting market decline, or the derivative bubble of 2007–2008 and the resulting Great Recession. What we do know is that putting a lot of money in one investment or even one type of investment is risky, and so is putting money in investments that do not pay an income.

Selling the Brooklyn Bridge

While the idea of spending ten times someone's annual income on a single tulip bulb seems ludicrous today (and rightly so), it is equally preposterous to think of selling the Brooklyn Bridge. Yet the sad truth is that it has been sold more than once—as has the Eiffel Tower.

In 1925, Victor Lustig sold the Eiffel tower twice. According to Brad Smithfield of Vintage News, Lustig got the idea of scamming investors when he was in Paris reading a newspaper about how the repairs and maintenance on the Eiffel Tower were so expensive that the government could not afford the upkeep.[7] To capitalize on this information, Lustig obtained a false letterhead from the City of Paris, falsified documents, and detailed a demolition plan for the Eiffel Tower. He posed as a government official, appointing himself the "Director General of the Ministere do Postes et Telegraphes," invited five scrap-metal business owners to a quiet meeting, and told them that the government was going to sell the Eiffel Tower—over seven thousand tons of metal—to metal scrappers. He told them to keep this meeting secret because the city was not ready for the negative press.

Of these five business owners, Lustig targeted André Poisson, as he was new to the metal scrapping industry. Lustig proceeded to tell Poisson that to gain rights to the Eiffel Tower he needed to pay up front $70,000 in cash—over $1.14 million in today's money. André Poisson made the payment and never saw Lustig again. Apparently, Lustig fled to Austria as soon as he got that cash. Poisson, too embarrassed to let the world know that he had fallen into Lustig's trap, never reported the scam to the police or the press—allowing Lustig to come back to Paris six months later and sell the Eiffel Tower again. This time, however, his scam was reported to the police and the press. The story got a lot of attention, and Lustig fled to the United States where, after several more scams, he was imprisoned. He died in Springfield, Missouri, on March 11, 1947.

A similar scam was undertaken by the infamous American conman George C. Parker, who is perhaps best known for "selling" the Brooklyn Bridge to unsuspecting immigrants not just once but several times. Many buyers even tried to erect toll booths on the bridge before they were removed by police. Throughout his career George Parker successfully "sold" multiple public landmarks, including Madison Square Garden, the Metropolitan Museum of Art, Grant's Tomb, and the Statue of Liberty.

A lesson that some people never seem to learn is that if something seems too good to be true, it probably is.

The Fyre Festival

We know that only about one in ten new ventures is successful in the short run (three years or less). We know that doctors, attorneys, investment advisors, salesmen, and other professionals spend years developing their practice to a point that they can call it a success. In most of these cases, building the practice takes more than three years. Why then do we expect a new venture to be successful?

It is unreasonable to believe that a busy kiosk in a shopping mall will develop into a competitor to Dillard's, Walmart, or Target in a matter of months. However, we see many anxious investors put money into new ventures and expect short-term success.

We could list hundreds of ventures in which investors have lost millions of dollars. But here, let's take a look at just one venture in which many major investors spent large amounts of money on a project that seemingly had all the elements of success. The Fyre Festival was planned by businessman Billy McFarland and rapper Ja Rule for six days on the Bahamian island of Great Exuma. In total, over $27 million was paid by investors to provide accommodations, food, and entertainment for the spectators.[8] Thousands of people opted in to this event for over $12,000 per couple. Tickets for the festival went for prices from $500 to $100,000. Yet, when guests arrived on the island, they were shocked to find that there was no music, no amenities, and no organization to provide for the thousands who had spent their money to attend the event.

Investors in the Fyre Festival lost all their money, and various lawsuits were filed against the organizers.

Celebrities Who Lost It All

Our society's infatuation with entertainers, including in sports, music, and acting has created income levels for those people that are many times that of the average worker and even that of the majority of successful business executives. It is disappointing, however, to see how poorly many of these people have handled their good fortunes and, in many cases, blown it all.

Many articles have been written on how athletes and other celebrities have lost their fortunes, and they often list the same names over and over. On November 2, 2018, *Entertainment Tonight* ran a story called "50 Celebrities Who Went Broke." A similar article was published by *Business Insider* on June 8, 2019, titled "25 Celebrities Who Were Rich and Famous Before Losing Their Money." A *Work + Money* piece titled "30 Celebs Who Made & Lost a Ton of Money" went live on September 30, 2021. *Moneywise* produced a story called "24 NFL Stars That Lost Millions of Dollars" in 2022, and *Money Inc.* updated a story in 2024 titled "20 High Paid Athletes Who Went Completely Broke."

My reason for bringing up these failures is to highlight the discipline needed to take care of the money you earn. I want to seriously emphasize the importance of the lessons you will learn throughout this book. The stories below recount how many very successful people have lost their fortunes by making serious mistakes in their disciplines.

Vince Young

I had the good fortune of seeing Vince Young play in the 2006 Rose Bowl national championship game between the University of Texas and University of Southern California. After graduating, he went on to sign a rookie contract in the NFL for a guaranteed $26 million. Yet in 2012, Fox Sports ran a story titled "How Did Vince Young End Up Broke?" He had filed for bankruptcy in 2014 and listed his assets as low as $500,000.[9] The Celebrity Net Worth website listed his net worth in 2023 at $400,000. We can only hope that the real number is higher than that.

This story is repeated again and again in sports. *Sports Illustrated* reported in 2009 that 78 percent of all NFL contract players are broke or financially stressed within two years of retiring from the NFL—and 60 percent of NBA players experience the same fate within five years of retirement.[10]

There is no financial skill required to take care of a million dollars that is not needed for your everyday living expenses. There is, however, a discipline required to protect those dollars against frivolous invest-ments. An outsider might say, "Just put it in a bank account," and that would be preferable to how many high earners handle their money. A wealthy person does not need to gamble, be greedy, or achieve excessive returns. A wealthy person needs only to achieve a decent return in order to have a bright future and maintain a high standard of living.

Michael Jackson

One of the most successful music artists of all time, Michael Jackson sold over 61 million albums and earned hundreds of millions of dollars during his career.

In 1988, Jackson bought a 2500-acre ranch in Santa Barbara. He named the ranch Neverland, and the property became world-famous, yet in 2008 the property was lost in foreclosure due to unpaid debts. Following the pop star's death in 2009, *Billboard* ran an article that reviewed Jackson's career, his successes and his failures. They reported that he had died at age fifty with $400 million in unpaid debt, and that he was spending $20 to $30 million per year more than he earned.[11] In February of 2014, investment banker David Dunn testified in court that he was owed more than $300,000 by Michael Jackson, and that the IRS was considering a tax bill of up to one billion dollars in unpaid taxes. He also told the court that the Jackson estate was virtually worthless.[12]

In a true case of being worth more dead than alive, the Jackson estate today is worth millions—yet just how many millions is unclear. We know that Sony paid $750 million for the rights to Jackson's music, but how much of that went and will go to the IRS has been a continuing battle.

M. C. Hammer

The rap star M. C. Hammer was worth more than $33 million at the height of his career. He spent money on fancy cars, airplanes, and a $30-million-dollar home, but filed for bankruptcy in 1996.[13] Despite earning continuing revenue from his music, in 2023 his net worth was only about $2 million, according to Celebrity Net Worth.

Heidi Montag

According to the TheThings website, Heidi Montag and her husband Spencer Pratt held a similar net worth of over $10 million at the peak of their careers.[14] Despite making over $2 million a year at one point, they were reportedly living rent free in a home owned by Pratt's parents later in life, and the couple's combined net worth was reported by *Life & Style* to be less than $300,000.[15]

Gary Busey

Gary Busey made his fortune by starring in the films *A Star is Born*, *The Buddy Holly Story*, *Silver Bullet*, *Point Break*, *Under Siege*, and *Lethal Weapon*, among others. After two divorces, reported bouts with cocaine and alcohol, and lavish spending, he filed for chapter 7 bankruptcy in

2012, listing $26,000 in assets, $57,000 in debts and $451,000 in taxes due.[16] His net worth today is reported by Celebrity Net Worth to be around $500,000.

Evander Holyfield

Evander Holyfield, a world-champion boxer, defeated Mike Tyson for the World Heavyweight title in 1996. *AP News* reported that Holyfield earned in excess of $120 million during his career.[17] The same article reported that his total earnings could be as high as $500 million, and that the "Famous Bite" fight alone earned him $34 million.

Holyfield went on to purchase an Atlanta mansion that reportedly had 109 rooms, but the athlete defaulted on his mortgage in 2008, and his landscaping company sued him for $550,000 in unpaid services. How did he lose all that money? We know that lavish spending, multiple wives, and several child support payments played a big part. Plus, the British publication *The Independent* reported in 2012 that Holyfield lost a fortune at casinos in Las Vegas and Atlantic City,[18] and the online publication *Grunge* reports that he dropped most of his dollars betting on sports events.[19] Celebrity Net Worth reports his net worth at $1 million, and other sites like The Richest have listed it at as low as $500,000.

Lindsay Lohan

Lindsay Lohan has also made millions of dollars throughout her career. Celebrity Net Worth reported her net worth to be over $27 million at one time, and at the peak of her fame she was offered $7.5 million per film. However, her finances suffered from overspending, drug addiction, and multiple rehab visits, per the *HuffPost*.[20]

On May 8, 2021, the *Richest* ran an article titled "Falling from Grace: How Lindsay Lohan Lost Millions."[21] The article relates the movie star's lavish lifestyle: She bought purses worth $12,000 to $20,000 each, one of which she is said to have put $1 million worth of jewelry in—and then misplaced. Lohan owed $100,000 to a limousine service and was sued by a tanning salon over a $40,000 debt. *TMZ* reported that the IRS seized her bank accounts in 2012 to settle her debts.[22]

Yahoo! reported in 2022 that Lohan's net worth was down to around $1.5 million.[23]

Dennis Rodman

Dennis Rodman played for eleven different NBA teams, including the Chicago Bulls during their three NBA championships, and earned $27 million during his basketball career.[24] He went on to make an additional million in the pro-wrestling arena, alongside his sponsorships, book sales, endorsements, and other sources of income. To stay enormously wealthy, all he had to do was bank some of those earnings. But it was not to be.

Along came Peggy Ann Fulford, advertising a degree from Harvard Law School, Wall Street success, and special expertise in helping athletes manage their money.[25] She enticed Dennis Rodman, Rickey Williams, and other successful athletes to trust her with all their earnings and wealth. She gave monthly allowances to her clients and supposedly deposited the balance of their money in a separate account—all "free of charge."

But were the assets deposited with a major investment firm that was a member of the DTC? No! Was the cash deposited in the owner's name with FDIC insurance? No! A large amount of the cash went directly into Fulford's own accounts, and then into different mysterious accounts with various titles.

Finally, Fulford's actions were called into question and things began to unravel. She was indicted in 2016, found guilty of fraud, and sentenced in 2018 to ten years in prison. Upon her sentencing she was required to pay $5.7 million in restitution to her victims.

A 2012 *AP News* article reported that Rodman appeared in an Orange County court to settle an $850,000 debt to his ex-wife, and that his lawyer claimed he was completely broke and unable to pay.[26]

After all of the millions he earned, the Celebrity Net Worth website listed Rodman's net worth at just $500,000 in 2024.

While Peggy Fulford was the major culprit in Rodman's massive losses, he was also well-known for his excessive spending habits, using his wealth to finance multiple piercings, legal issues, substance use and rehab, a hit-and-run accident, and two trips to North Korea in 2013 and 2017. Rodman has certainly led a colorful life, but if he had put just a fraction of his earnings into reasonable investments, he would be worth a great deal of money today.

The Theranos Inc. Meltdown

Like many other scams, Theranos was several years in the making. The company was founded in 2003 by nineteen-year-old college-dropout Elizabeth Holmes as a health-technology company. The firm was promoted as a state-of-the-art blood-testing company, with proponents touting the company's ability to complete more than 240 tests from just a few drops of blood. Over $900 million was raised from investors, and many famous names were included in the early shareholder list. Over $700 million of this capital was raised without the investors receiving statements from an independent auditor.[27]

In 2014, *Forbes* magazine listed Holmes as one of the 400 richest Americans, estimating her net worth at around $4.5 billion.[28] The magazine also named her the "world's youngest self-made woman billionaire."[29] She appeared in the billionaire lists, and Theranos was valued at over $9 billion—before the technology was questioned.[30]

In June of 2015, Blue Cross of Pennsylvania chose Theranos as its primary blood-testing facility. Yet on October 14, 2015, the *Wall Street Journal* ran an article questioning the effectiveness of Theranos's testing.[31] The stock price of the company began to decline, and deterioration accelerated after that.

The company was dissolved in 2018.

In 2021, COO Ramesh Balwani was convicted on twelve charges of fraud and sentenced to thirteen years in prison, while Elizabeth

Holmes was found guilty on four counts of fraud the following year. She was sentenced to eleven years in prison.[32]

Don't Risk It All

This chapter could go on for thousands of pages. Fortunes blown by popular and presumably responsible people could fill thousands of pages, but simple discipline can help us avoid these colossal mistakes. One simple practice that goes far is avoiding illiquid investments: There is no liquidity in a lottery ticket. There is no liquidity in money sent to an unknown investor. There is no liquidity in a private venture, investing in an entertainment event, or lending money to a relative.

We all know within a reasonable estimate what we are worth in dollars. Only a portion of that net worth can be considered our long-term money—we should never risk it all on any one undiversified investment.

Chapter 4

Poor Strategies to Avoid

In this chapter, we will cover all of the investing strategies that you should *not* follow. These are mistakes that you must avoid at all costs! You may notice that this chapter is the longest in this book, and there's a good reason for that. As we have seen again and again, the secret to being financially comfortable is not making big profits with risky stock picks or any other get-rich-quick scheme. Avoiding strategies that will *lose* your money is way more important than finding ways to acquire it. Here are the strategies you must avoid.

Concentrated Positions

Having concentrated positions means that a large portion of your investments are concentrated in a particular company or sector of the economy, and it is critical that you do not put yourself in this situation. There are countless stories of once-successful companies that have fallen on hard times. Whether a business fails because of bad management or changes in the economy, an overinvestment in that organization will ruin the performance of any portfolios concentrated there.

The Dow Jones index is a list of the thirty most prominent companies in the United States. In its history, going back to 1896, the index has included American Sugar, Bethlehem Steel, Chrysler, U.S. Leather, U.S. Rubber, American Cotton Oil, Tennessee Coal, Westinghouse Electric, Eastman Kodak, Nash Motors, Sears Roebuck, Woolworth, International Harvester, General Electric, JCPenney, and Xerox. All these names have disappeared from the index—most have disappeared entirely, and the majority have declared bankruptcy at one time or another.

My intention here is not to highlight the failures of major companies but to underline the extreme importance of diversifying your investments. The majority of successful companies will provide good results for a long, long time. However, let us consider two companies that today's investors may remember—Eastman Kodak and General Electric (GE). Both of these companies were part of the Nifty Fifty, a stock group developed in the 1960s and '70s when the markets were locked in a trading zone, or a narrow range of stock prices without growth.

Eastman Kodak became the world's leading camera company in the 1970s when it obtained an 85 percent market share in that industry. Its stock traded at prices in the '70s and '80s in 1976 and 1978. But when the camera market changed with the advent of digital cameras and phone cameras, the stock was trading at under $1 in 2011. Eastman Kodak filed for bankruptcy in 2012 and later emerged from bankruptcy to operate as a skeleton of its old company.

Many analysts called GE the world's best managed company. Indeed, it became one of the largest companies in the world and was regularly seen as the icon of American business. The stock traded at an adjusted (for splits) price of $3 in 1980 but rose to $256 in 2000. But in 2001, Jeffery Immelt took over the company as CEO, and things began to unravel. The price of GE went from $256 in 2000 to less than $50 in 2009. Anyone who was concentrated in GE stock in 2000 and held it for the long haul would have had a horrible twenty years in their portfolio. The market recovery took GE back up, but when Immelt left in 2017 the stock was still worth less than $200, a decline of almost 20 percent, over a period when the stock market had gained well over 200 percent. My intention here is not to judge the brilliance of Jack Welch, the previous CEO of GE, against that of Immelt but convey how good companies fare over time and in different economic conditions—and why diversification is extremely important in a portfolio.

But here's another caveat. In the quest for diversification, many investors will make investments in a hasty manner. Some of these investments are highly touted as "alternative investments." Returns on alternative investments can vary from extraordinary to dismal, and the average investor is not equipped to evaluate them—even professionals will have variable records. In 2017, the *Dallas Morning News* ran an article about problems that had occurred with the city's police and firemen's pension fund.[1] The managers of the fund had assumed over an 8 percent return on the fund's assets, but the actual long-term returns were much less. Managers of the fund had turned to alternative investments and, between 2003 and 2011, the alternative investments in this fund of around $3.5 billion increased from around $300 million to $1.3 billion. At the lows, more than a third of these funds were invested in illiquid investments. The recession of 2008–2009 brought major real estate prices down over 40 percent—one property in the Arizona desert was shown declining from $27.2 million to $7.5 million. The Dallas police, the Dallas firemen, the Dallas city council, and even the Texas legislature were all drawn into finding solutions for this underfunded pension plan.

This lesson on concentrated positions plays out again and again, with people reacting poorly when they find out that they may be concentrating their money in the wrong places. One of the best examples I have seen was a study by the Kemper Funds, part of Kemper Insurance, which is now part of the Zurich Insurance Group. The study was published way back on May 31, 1994, and was titled "Client Behavior 101."[2] It listed the prominent 219 growth funds existing at that time, which returned an annual rate of +12.5% over the five-year period of the study—and yet the investors in those funds had a net annual loss of -2.2%. It's a real shame that a fund group can have a five-year record of double-digit returns while the average investor experiences a net loss. There are several lessons to be learned from this study: One is that the higher the return for an investment category, the higher the likely volatility of that investment. Another lesson is that investors are more likely to sell into serious declines. (The more diversified the investor, though, the less likely that person will sell into those declines.) Finally, patience is extremely important for successful long-term investing.

Another important point to consider in regard to diversification is growth stocks versus value stocks. While growth has held a slight edge over value in the last several decades, the volatility of growth stocks has been extremely large. The tech bubble of 2000 is a good example. Many of the developing tech companies of the late '90s were in the capital-weighted NASDAQ index, which was represented by the Invesco QQQ ETF. The price of the QQQ hit 107 in February of 2000, and the NASDAQ index reached a high of 109 that year. The tech stocks averaged a P/E (price-to-earnings) ratio of almost 100 at the year 2000 peak, and investors continued buying them with both hands. That peak was followed by what has been called "the Tech Wreck"—a period when tech stocks adjusted from those extreme highs. The QQQ would not return to that level again until the first quarter of 2015, a fifteen-year period. And the NASDAQ declined from its 109-point high to a low of 21 over the next two years. It would be fifteen years before that index reached another new high.

The main lesson from this example is that one index does not provide a lot of diversification—especially if that index is the QQQ. A weighted index does not provide an investor with much diversification because the value of the largest stocks can be as much as seventy times the value of the smallest. At the time of this writing, tech stocks accounted for half of the QQQ value, while the index contained ten different sectors with one hundred stocks—and the largest stock in the index was two hundred times the value and weight of the smallest. An investment in the QQQ has always been tech-heavy, subject to extreme fluctuation, and this is a trend that continues today. It is not advisable to put a total portfolio in the QQQ, but participation in the QQQ can add a growth component to your investments.

In the decade leading up to the peak in 2021, stocks making up the FAANG index—Facebook, Apple, Amazon, Netflix, and Google—were all the rage. While the charts show only about a 46 percent decline in the index (5,821 to 3,183), the different stocks bottomed out at different times, and the temptation to sell was huge. Google declined from a high of $148 to $88 (40 percent), Facebook from $379 to $93 (75 percent), Netflix from $690 to $175 (75 percent), Amazon from $175 to $84 (50 percent), and Apple, the most stable of the group, from $178 to $130 (25 percent). Very few people who bought stocks near the peaks held them through the decline of 2022.

Investing in growth can be a valuable part of an investment strategy, but overinvesting can be a major problem. It's impossible to know when a growth stock will lose its luster and cease its rapid growth. Sometimes growth outperforms value, and sometimes value outperforms growth. The extreme volatility of growth stocks makes the temptation to go all out extremely dangerous when markets decline—growth stocks can rise rapidly during good times but fall just as fast during corrections. Maintaining proper diversification allows you to participate in growth but also wade through the bad times without major losses.

In May of 2023, the top seven stocks of the S&P index were very positive for the year, but the overall balance of the index was negative. By the end of the year, the index was slightly positive. At that time the largest stocks were over 400 times the value of the smallest. *This was not diversification.* When 7 stocks determine the direction of an index while the remaining 493 show an average in the other direction, it's a mockery of diversification. Often in my career, I've heard from clients that their best strategy is to just buy the S&P and look away. I would remind them about the fifteen years that the QQQ spent wandering in the desert before it turned positive at the beginning of the century. Take a look at the trajectory of the price of the QQQ on the chart below.

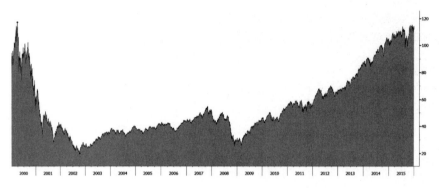

The price of the QQQ ETF 2000–2015. Courtesy of Bloomberg L.P.

If you are invested exclusively in ETFs and mutual funds, it is paramount that you have some diversification in the investment group that includes growth, value, and dividends—that means ETFs or mutual funds of more than one index or group of stocks.

The Nifty Fifty

Unusual times will often bring about some unusual movement in the stock markets. During the hyperinflation period of the 1970s, the "Nifty Fifty" was a go-to list that all the astute investors supposedly owned. It was hyped as a list of companies that would insure against high inflation, because these companies produced goods and services that are sold at higher prices—razors and blades by Gillette, for example, were expected to keep up with inflation. The P/E ratio of the Nifty Fifty varied a lot, but it was above forty for several years and even rose above fifty-five for a period of time, while the balance of the stock market traded below ten for much of that time period. Were the high prices of the Nifty Fifty justified? Probably not entirely, but over the long term that list did outperform much of the market.

So what happened to the Nifty Fifty? Some of the companies were bought out by other entities: Lubrizol was sold to Berkshire, which has owned it for decades now. Squibb sold out to Pabst Brewing. Upjohn to Pfizer. Avon Products sold to Natura & Co. and became a private company. Schering sold to Merk in 2009. Gillette sold to Proctor and Gamble. Heublein sold to multiple companies. International Telephone and Telegraph (ITT) became a conglomerate and then split, selling various parts to many entities.

Amp, a major electrical parts maker, failed to transition to a new technology and was bought by Tyco in 1999, then sold to TE Connectivity in 2011 and resold to Commscope in 2015—a small part of its original self. Xerox floundered when the internet came into existence. Eastman Kodak faded away when the iPhone and digital cameras took over the industry. Polaroid declined about the same time that new technology began to capture the Eastman Kodak business. Digital Equipment was sold to Compaq in 1998 and then sold off in parts as the computer industry transformed. Simplicity Patterns sold to CSS Industries in 2017 after the digital age began to replace manual operations. Burroughs went to Sperry in 1986 and was then sold to Unisys, whose stock was under $5 at the time of this writing.

Then there were some companies in the Nifty Fifty that experienced outright failures. JCPenney filed for bankruptcy in 2020. S. S. Kresge became Kmart, which became part of Sears, which failed in 2018. MGIC Investment Corp filed for bankruptcy and was eventually liquidated. Revlon filed for bankruptcy and became a penny stock trading over the counter.

The survivors of this group carried the load and made the Nifty Fifty an ultimate success, outperforming the Dow Jones index by a small amount over the succeeding years. The surviving stocks included Philip Morris, Proctor & Gamble, Pfizer, PepsiCo, Bristol-Meyers, Merck, GE, Eli Lilly, American Home Products, Johnson & Johnson, Anheuser-Busch, Citi, Schlumberger, McDonald's, Walt Disney, Dow, American Express, Texas Instruments, International

Flavors & Fragrances, Halliburton, Baxter, IBM, Philip Morris, and Coca-Cola.

These surviving stocks carried the entire original Nifty Fifty list of stocks. While there were many mergers, sellouts, and failures in the group, the net performance over the succeeding years was very good. The majority of long-term, successful corporate stories involve development and growth over a long time, and that is certainly the case with the Nifty Fifty survivors. Major companies can and will fail—a fact that highlights the extreme importance of diversifying your investments.

Trading

A well-known saying in financial circles states, "There are old traders and there are bold traders, but there are no old, bold traders."

We are not talking about the trading desks of investment houses and corporations, which exist for the sole purpose of buying and selling stocks for investment firms or commodities for producing corporations. We are talking about traders who propose to make money buying and selling the short-term moves of stocks, commodities, or other assets.

Money magazine ran a story about two University of California professors, Terrance Odean and Brad Barber, who conducted a multiyear study in the 1990s on the trading habits of eighty thousand investors—a huge sample, in terms of studies of this sort.[3] The results broke down perfectly, showing that the most active traders achieved the worst market performance. The least active group achieved returns of 18.5 percent annualized over the period, the next least active, 17.6 percent, then 16.8, 15.3, and 11.4 percent for the most active.

The *Wall Street Journal* reported the results of the ProShares UltraShort fund that had declined 75 percent in the year 2021.[4] Under these conditions, a 75 percent gain is only a small fraction of the loss—the gain required to offset a 75 percent loss is 357 percent.

We all want to buy stocks that have fallen too far and too fast, and we want to sell shares of companies that have risen astronomically.

Those moves, however, are hard for the average investor to time. They can be losers in the short run, and even if they are timed correctly, the returns on those moves can be a long time coming.

A favorite quote of Benjamin Graham, one of the all-time most successful money managers, is "You can't time the market." Graham spent much of his early career trying to develop a formula for when to enter and exit the market, and his ultimate conclusion was that it is impossible to time the market. Yes, you can change allocations depending upon the levels of the market, but timing the market is virtually impossible. In other words, short-term trading is not for the average investor, and it is questionable even for the professional. Rather than trying to time the market, you should buy and hold onto good stocks or good funds. That is how you can benefit from the long-term upward trend in the value of stocks, as illustrated by the chart below, showing growth in the Dow Jones index over the past century.

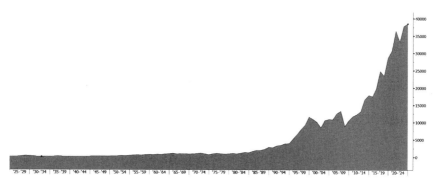

Dow Jones index 1924–2024. Courtesy of Bloomberg L.P.

Derivatives

Derivatives can be explained in several different ways, but the simple definition is any investment item beyond (that is, derived from) the actual security—whether it be a stock, a bond, a CD, or a produced commodity. The first derivative on stocks and bonds is an ETF or a mutual fund, and these are proper items for a conservative investor to own. Investing in almost any derivative beyond these, such as options, commodities, or credit default swaps, would be considered trading and involve more risk. In almost all of these cases, an individual investor is competing with professionals who are buying and selling these assets for use in their business. The bottom line is that any derivatives beyond ETFs and mutual funds are high-risk investments that you should avoid.

Commodities

When it comes to commodities trading, a typical investor has very little information on what is happening in any given commodity. In contrast, a purchase desk at one of the food companies can have crop data from several sources on wheat, corn, and oats. They can also have various files on the weather in all the areas producing said crops. A commodity contract will normally require only about a 10 percent deposit against the total—that means that the investor is putting up only one-tenth of the exposure but is taking ten times the risk on any move in that commodity, and any individual investor is competing against major consuming companies. For example, If I buy a crude oil contract, I am competing against companies like ExxonMobil, Chevron, and Marathon, which buy these contracts to use the crude oil in their refineries. Trading in commodities is so risky that it should be considered only by professionals.

Cryptocurrencies

There seems to be more questions about cryptocurrencies than there are answers, and it may be years before we have a good understanding of where these things fit in the financial system. One of the main draws for using cryptocurrency has been the ability to shield transactions from public view, and they have consequently been welcomed by drug cartels and other illegal organizations that must conceal their money movements from authorities.

Cryptocurrency is made possible through blockchain technology, an innovative and advanced database system that allows for the transparent recording and sharing of information across a peer-to-peer network. I won't try to explain the technology in detail, but there are a few facts you should know: first, blockchain itself is not a currency, but rather the process used for crypto transactions; second, the blockchain processing centers use a huge amount of electricity; and third, there are many other many possible uses of blockchain that have nothing to do with cryptocurrencies.

Bitcoin, currently the most popular cryptocurrency, is extremely volatile in comparison to the stable value of the U.S. Dollar. The U.S. Dollar Index (DXY) chart below shows about a 15 percent variation in the last ten years from the 100 level, a total range of about 30 percent, while the Bitcoin chart, also below, ranges from under 200 to over 7,000—a range of over 33,500 percent! The volatility in the largest digital currency has been over 1,100 times that of the U.S. Dollar. Since your objective should be to minimize the volatility of your assets, digital currencies should be left to the professionals.

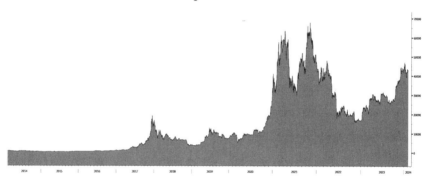

The value of Bitcoin 2014–2024. Courtesy of Bloomberg L.P.

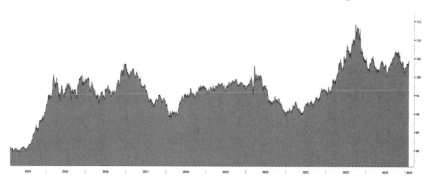

U.S. Dollar Index 2014–2024. Courtesy of Bloomberg L.P.

Genius Claims and Magic Formulas

We've all seen the commercials, read the ads, and heard all about the extremely successful formulas for making quick money while avoiding the associated risks. "These systems were developed by investing geniuses! You're simply foolish if you choose not to participate in these proven techniques."

The reality is if there were any magic formulas or techniques for investing, all the major investment firms would be using them.

It's been said that the best way to succeed in market forecasting is to make so many forecasts that, in the future, odds are that at least one of those forecasts was accurate. In one bear-market year, I remember the Mansfield Chart Service running an article on forecasting in which they referenced an extremely cautious stance on the market. Despite this language, they could not find any original quotation from that source about caution on the market. Another quote they ran from a different source mentioned a 10 percent market correction back in January, but when they checked the actual quotation, it read something like, "While we foresee the possibility of market corrections of as much as 10%, we strongly believe the overall thrust of the market is upward." In other words, forecasting is futile.

There is a barometer called "The Sky-Is-Falling Index"—a contrary measurement of stock prices. This barometer shows how the general public's prevailing attitude on the stock market is often inverse what actually occurs. Excessive enthusiasm often precedes a market top, while excessive pessimism usually precedes a bottom. Buying equities when the index is low and raising cash when it's high is always a good strategy, but that's not some supposed genius's secret system or a magic formula. It's just a case of applying common sense to publicly available data.

My point here is that you shouldn't get too excited about any investing techniques except for long-term, steady growth in the bottom line. And I remind you that to benefit from steady growth, you have to be patient through major declines in the market.

Time and again we see reports on wonderful investment formulas that protect us from loss and give us maximum participation in the stock market. My favorite statement on this subject comes from Anthony W. Tabell of Delafield, Harvey, Tabell, Inc., who said that "most formulas fail because they tend to lock the barn after the horse has been stolen."

The basic facts remain the same: bear markets occur when the brilliant market investors fail to see some hidden risk, and then bull markets tend to bring the averages back to some reasonable price. We have over four hundred years of public market history showing the average returns on stocks to be about 10 percent annually and the return on borrowed money to be around 5 percent. These records go back to the 1700s, way before the United States became a country. If there had been, at any time, any magic formula for outperforming the massive fluctuations of stock prices and interest rates, it would have revealed itself long before now.

Reasonable investment practice dictates that we ignore hype and claims of magic formulas and look for long-term returns to grow our investments.

Falling for magic formulas is an example of what you might call ignoring reality. Major moves in the stock market have always been followed by major corrections—statistics tell us that the market goes up an average of two out of every three years, and that means that the market is down one of every three years. But it can be hard to accept that reality when the actual year-to-year cycles do not adhere to this average but vary by large amounts. For example, the market increased fivefold between 1987 to 1999. Then the following bear market of 2000 to 2002 returned prices to the long-term average. That process is called reverting to the mean or, in simple terms, returning to the average. In the long term, the four-hundred-year average return on equities (stocks) is approximately 10 percent annually, while borrowed money averages about 5 percent. These numbers can urge us to invest all our money in stocks with enthusiasm, but in reality, the bear markets that look short on paper can last years before prices return to the norm. We can enjoy successes when the markets are going up, but we must expect corrections. And to be successful, we must invest for the long term.

In 1987, we experienced the largest one-day drop in market history. I had multiple concerned clients in my office that day, but I did not sell a single share of stock during the day's trading. The Dow Jones index closed down 22.6 percent, after being down 25 percent at its worst. Few investors would have guessed it, but the Dow Jones index would go on to close up for the year of 1987. That was a clear example of holding good securities through bad markets.

Penny Stocks

Penny stocks are usually defined as stocks selling under $1 per share. There are, however, many restrictions by government agencies and major firms that prevent you from buying stocks below $5 with borrowed money. Stocks that fall below $5 in price have drifted into a category where a lot of their buying power—including cash, cash equivalent, and available margin—has gone away. Responsible CEOs of respectable firms will generally avoid having company shares fall into this category. If such a price event occurs for a firm with a good balance sheet, the board will often approve a reverse split, or a consolidation of existing shares into fewer shares at a higher price, in order to bring the stock price over the $5 level.

To be marginable—eligible to be bought on margin, with borrowed money—stocks must trade on a national stock exchange, either the NYSE or the NASDAQ. At the time of this writing, there were about seven thousand of those companies. To be listed on either exchange, a company must satisfy certain listing requirements, including solvency, an initial stock price above $5, being current with financial reports, publishing audited reports regularly (at least twice per year), and meeting minimal capital requirements.

Stocks selling under $1 are a different story. Stocks at this price are traded on what is called the OTCBB market, an abbreviation for the Over-the-Counter Bulletin Board, and there are at least twelve thousand companies in this market. Most companies listed on the OTCBB do not meet the listing requirements of the major exchanges for a number of different reasons, yet those requirements are extremely important. If financial data is not available to investment professionals, then there is no way for individuals to have the information necessary to make good investment decisions.

Many big profits can be made in the buying and selling of these stocks, but the risks are extremely high and often don't pay off. For one, the visibility of earnings and sales is poor and very often unaudited. The spread between the bid and ask is also very often high, and the commissions are very expensive on these items. For example, the undiscounted commission on eight thousand shares of a 50-cent stock is listed by one firm as $170. On a $4,000 transaction, that commission is 4.25 percent of the investment, so that the round-turn amount (the amount earned by selling the investment) would be 8.5 percent—which is about the average annual investment return on an investment account. But the average spread between the bid and the asked price on a 50-cent stock is over 5 cents, raising that round-turn cost to over 20 percent of the price. We can therefore characterize the investment in these penny stocks as trading, speculating, gambling, or all of the above.

All of the major investment firms have restrictions on buying penny stocks. Some prohibit them entirely, some restrict investments to a small percent of the account, such as 5 percent, and others only to accounts of $1 million or more. In all those cases, the intent is to shield the investor from losing a large portion of their money to this kind of investment.

Lending and Borrowing

The absolute first consideration when making any loan is to evaluate the likelihood of getting the money back. On a scale of 1 to 10, what are the chances? If lending to a relative, it's a sad statistic that your chances of getting your money back are 50 percent or less.

In many cases, a person who would never put a sum of money into a single illiquid investment will loan a friend, neighbor, or relative that same amount of money without documentation or even a firm agreement on the repayment process. Repayment of a loan from a close relative is never an easy discussion, but it should be approached in a formal manner to protect your assets.

Many years ago, I lent $4,000 to my daughter and son-in-law for a partial down payment on a house. In order to simplify the accounting process, we agreed that the repayment deposits would go into a mutual fund, because the records are clear of distortion if no other transactions are made in the account. The loan was repaid with deposits to that mutual fund over the next three years, and I said, jokingly, that I never intended to sell that position. To date, I have not sold any of that fund, and now the position is worth more than $40,000—which the mutual fund company has delightedly used as an example for their marketing efforts. There is a significant lesson in this story: any loan has a significant bearing upon your future net worth. My loan to my relatives was paid off properly, however, without that loan repayment, my balance sheet today would be at least $40,000 less.

We see a lot of advertisements telling us to "buy now and pay later." This is, pure and simple, borrowing money—otherwise known as going into debt. Some of these ads will give us two years of no principal or interest payments. Let's look at what happens if I spend $10,000 on a project with no payments for two years. In many cases the interest is 10 percent or more. Using the 10 percent rate, by the time I start paying, the total bill starts at $12,000—up a significant amount from the $10,000 start. The monthly payments on a three-year payout would be $387.21, for a total of $13,939.56, including $3,939.56 of interest. If I had started paying the loan off at the time of purchase, two years earlier, my monthly payment would be $322.53, and I would pay a total of $11,611.08, including $1,611.08 of interest. Better yet, if I had not borrowed the $10,000 in the first place—if, for example, I had been able to pay for my emergency roof replacement out of my emergency savings account—I would have no payments and pay zero interest.

The Consumer Financial Protection Bureau did a study in 2022 that showed 62 percent of all Buy Now Pay Later (BNPL) borrowers use credit cards on major purchases versus 44 percent of non-BNPL consumers.[5] This study shows that almost 50 percent more BNPL buyers are borrowing money with credit cards. Credit card interest rates, of course, are far higher than 10 percent, making credit card debt incredibly expensive.

The real lesson here is, if at all possible, pay as you go.

Putting Your Money in New Technology

A simple fact to remember when looking at any new technology is that the developer of a new product is almost never the same as the inventor.

Over my many years in the financial advising business, the most excited I ever saw investors was when they brought up the possibility of investing in some new technology. Any new technology will present a myriad of investment opportunities for investors to spend money for the advancement of the new invention. Investments in technology are especially attractive to investors because the technology sector is growing rapidly, and technology stocks have a huge growth potential due to the strong demand for products and services.

One of my wealthy clients began buying General Telephone and Electronics (GTE) stock in the late 1970s because the company had filed a patent on a flat-screen TV. The roots of GTE went way back to 1924 when Sylvania, which would eventually be a subsidiary of GTE, was formed to manufacture radio tubes for the growing radio industry. Sylvania became one of the industry leaders for TVs when the television industry began flourishing, and Sylvania TVs were popular with many households in the United States.

Yet GTE was sold to Verizon in June of 2000, and their flat screen TV was never marketed. Supposedly they had developed the technology, but it languished in production for many years. Before long, other companies began to enter the field, and virtually all the old TV manufacturers vanished by selling out or failing. Magnavox, Philco, RCA, Zenith, Motorola, GE, Sylvania, and Emerson were all popular television brands at one time . . . how many of those TVs do you see today?

Example #1: Autos

In the years 1900 through 1908, there were 480 companies producing automobiles. Many of them were public companies investors could buy stock in, yet only three of those would stick around for the next twenty years. The lesson here is that an early investor in one of the greatest inventions of all time would have had to be extremely precise in selecting the proper stock in order to make money.

I remember reading an article in the 1980s, published in a Dallas-specific magazine, that highlighted a local company producing electric cars. I faced pressure from an owner of this company to invest personal money in the firm because the new technology was "certain to flourish." Like most other new auto companies, the firm was later closed and liquidated. Over the next several years there were dozens of other start-up companies claiming to be developing "the electric car." It would be another thirty years before the first company, Tesla, would report a profit in this flourishing "new technology."

Example #2: Computers

The computer industry is a good example of how rapidly a new invention can change the landscape and how many companies can be involved in the development and marketing of a new invention—with so few good investments.

In the early days of computer production, there were as many as 150 computer manufacturers. Many of those were publicly traded companies, yet most ultimately failed at selling computers over the long haul.

IBM was one of these early computer manufacturers, and the IBM 360 was one of the first highly successful machines. Those early machines were filled with vacuum tubes and exuded a lot of heat—in college, I can remember walking by the building where a 360 ran all day, and the heat from the many exhaust fans would actually sting your skin if you got too close.

The invention of the semiconductor and circuit board greatly accelerated the development of computers. Some of the early solid-state computer manufacturers included Philco, Siemens, Sperry Rand, Honeywell, Olivetti, and Packard Bell.

As a student at the University of Texas School of Engineering, I helped with the preparations for an annual technology show that had become famous at the school. One year, the staff was laughing about something that had happened the day before when a young Sperry Rand salesman came into the office and asked to speak to the dean of the school. He excitedly told us that he had a closeout deal on two Sperry Rand computers at $25,000 each, and he was sure the dean would like to know about the deal. When we passed the model numbers on to the dean, he did not have time to talk to the sales rep and told him to just have the computers delivered. The salesman began to stutter, trying to explain why he needed to see the dean. What he did not know was that the evening before, a department meeting had authorized the purchase of two computers for the school—and the authorization had included that specific model of computer. The salesman was stunned, but his year just got a big boost—fifty thousand dollars was a lot of money in the 1950s. And Sperry Rand moved on to the next generation of computers.

Even as successful as IBM was in those early years, we can now look back on the times when it was not. The stock traded as high as $125 in 1999, yet twenty years later the stock could be purchased for just $100. In the meantime, a lot of dividends were paid out to investors, but the company was less than a stellar investment. There were a number of reasons for this dip, but it was primarily caused by the company's delayed adoption of cloud technology in the midst of the worldwide coronavirus pandemic. Few investors at the turn of the century expected IBM to go stagnant for more than twenty years, yet investors with a diversified portfolio were much happier than those who were concentrated in IBM stock. Good portfolio managers will keep track of company earnings and add or reduce positions as needed to adjust.

Example #3: Lasers

Development of the laser was spread over many years and involved many companies. Typical of new technologies, dozens of companies entered the field and filed hundreds of patents without any success. A 1996 report listed companies with names that you and I would find unrecognizable: Trumpf, Coherent, IPG, Han's Laser, II–VI, Lumentum, HGTech, Bystronic, Raycus, and Castech.[6]

Example #4: Wind Power

Wind farms have been appearing all over the world in recent years, and wind power is now producing about 7 percent of the electricity in the U.S. Yet wind turbine failures have also made many headlines. According to an article published in *Bloomberg*, the race to create bigger turbines is to blame for the increased manufacturing issues.[7] A study conducted by the U.S. Wind Energy Technologies Office found that the leading cause of wind turbine failures are cracks that form on the bearings in high- and intermediate-speeds, while the second leading cause is gear failures.[8] Well-known companies that have the biggest stake in wind power are Siemens, GE, and Mitsubishi, but there are many other companies that produce components or benefit from the industry. Anyone who is looking to invest in wind turbine technology or a similar innovation should be aware of the challenges and pitfalls associated with it.

Example #5: Marijuana

While cannabis is not an invention, legal marijuana is a new development in the investment world. New approvals of this use for cannabis have provided many opportunities for investment, but the industry is filled with farm, retail, and product failures by people and companies trying to capitalize on these opportunities. All of the original public pot-oriented company trading in the United States experienced a 90 percent or more decline from their high prices, and many went bankrupt.

Example #6: Solar Power

While solar power is a relatively new phenomenon, it appears to be here to stay as a source of electricity—the portion of world power coming from sunlight is now about 2 percent and growing. As with most new inventions, the development of solar power involved a lot of experiments at different companies and universities. The technology for solar energy originated with the invention of the photovoltaic cell, an electronic device that converts light energy directly into electricity, and its evolution has involved various types of panels and batteries.

Solar panels have been a popular way to produce electric power while the transition away from fossil fuels is taking place. It is important to note that many investments in these projects have been contributions to a cause and are not even close to wise investments. I do not want to advise against making a contribution of this sort, but before making any investments it is critical to consider the return and run the numbers. At the time of this writing, many projects in the solar energy space were eligible for government subsidies, making them a profitable venture. However, a large proportion of solar projects were not, and were therefore much riskier.

Several years ago, I ran the numbers for a lady who insisted that her solar-panel installation would make her money. She lived in a resort area of Mexico where there was no subsidy for solar power and, based on very optimistic projections from the power company, her break-even point for getting her principal back was twenty-two years. If she wanted even a 2 percent return (just equal to the Fed's target inflation rate) on the investment, she would have to live until she was 118 years old.

The relative costs of solar panels and equipment have been declining as manufacturers make progress in efficiency and productivity. Any investment in solar, however, should be evaluated carefully before putting money into it.

Primer for Chapters 5-6

Making Wise Investments

Moving on from what you should avoid when investing your money, we can now address the proper behaviors in making wise investments. New investors must always be diligent in the accumulation process while learning about proper investing. One of the most important topics we will cover in the coming chapters is managing interest rates. Whether we leave the management of our assets to a professional or retain portfolio management ourselves, we must adhere to the proper strategies. Once we have some money in savings, we can then begin to look at some other investment vehicles, like real estate or annuities. This section of the book will introduce some of those vehicles and how we should approach them, along with everything we should avoid.

In a world where we are constantly bombarded with flashy investment opportunities and the "next big idea," temptations to put our money in dangerous places and illiquid investments can distort our thinking—especially when they claim to return a lot of money.

Learning to move beyond the hype, attaining wisdom and practicing proper discipline, is absolutely necessary to become a successful investor.

Chapter 5

Make Interest Rates Work for You—Not against You

If you talk to any bank executive, you will hear the same thing over and over again: you should be a lender, not a borrower. Borrowing is sometimes justified, but most people do way too much of it—and they borrow money in the wrong way. In this chapter, I will explain the difference between proper and poisonous borrowing, as well as proper and poisonous lending.

When You Should Borrow

Virtually everyone needs a mortgage when buying a permanent place to live. There are many reasons one might decide to purchase a home—maybe you are expecting a child, or maybe you're just tired of paying rent. Most people want a place with multiple bedrooms, a large backyard for their children or pets, and a neighborhood where there are friendly neighbors. There are times, however, when this purchase should be delayed. There are houses available for lease in almost every neighborhood, and most apartments are offered for rent or lease. While it's true that the owner of any rental property will apply a markup to their total cost, most rental properties were purchased when interest rates were much less than their peaks. When rates are very high, many properties are available for a relatively reasonable lease because the landlord purchased it when rates—and possibly prices—were at lower levels. It is in times such as these that people who are anxious to buy a home might be better off renting or leasing instead.

During my career, I have seen mortgage rates as high at 18 percent (in 1981) and as low as 3 percent (in 2020). The long-term average is around 6 percent, but these cycles can last a long time. From 1978 until 1991, mortgage rates were above 9 percent; from 2012 until 2021, they were below 5. When rates are expected to decline, some people will buy a house on a five-year mortgage. Those mortgages are due in total after the five-year period, and the buyer must then start over with a new mortgage. Yet, if interest rates have gone up rather than down, those qualifying for a five-year mortgage might face higher rates when the five-year term expires.

So there are situations when borrowing money to buy a house is not a wise decision. But given the right circumstances—primarily that the costs of ownership are not significantly higher than the costs of renting—a home mortgage can be prudent. That will depend partly on how high or low interest rates are, which depends on the Federal Reserve.

Understand the Role of the Federal Reserve Bank

The Federal Reserve Bank, commonly known as the Fed, is the central bank of the United States and is in charge of the interest rate policies for the country—it is the most powerful central bank in the world. There are twelve Federal Reserve Bank locations, and each of these entities has a president. The most publicized responsibility of the Fed is setting the Effective Federal Funds Rate (or Fed funds), which is the rate charged by banks when they lend funds to each other overnight. If we asked ten people for the amount of this rate, probably nine of the ten would not have an answer, but the Fed funds rate is one of the most influential economic factors in the country, affecting most short- and long-term rates.

The Fed has a number of ways to control the economy, including setting monetary policy, monitoring the safety and soundness of financial institutions, fostering payment and settlements between institutions, and promoting consumer protection. These powers cover a broad range of actions, and we won't even try to get into all of them. The most significant role of the Fed is setting short-term interest rates, yet they also affect longer-term rates by buying and selling treasury securities, corporate bonds, and mortgage securities. At a peak in April of 2022, the Federal Reserve owned $8.96 trillion in bonds, including over 20 percent of all United States Treasury bonds that were outstanding at the time.

When You Shouldn't Borrow

Imprudent borrowing could very well have its own chapter, but to keep things simple, I will cover just a few general principles you should keep in mind: Avoid long-term borrowing, with the exception of mortgage loans when they are appropriate. Avoid high-interest loans, such as credit card debt. If at all possible, you should delay spending during high interest-rate periods.

Credit Cards

If you come away from this book with just one takeaway, make it this: never, ever carry credit card debt. The interest rate on credit cards is always several times higher than the interest on a bank loan, and it compounds every month. If you have credit card debt that will last more than a couple of months, look into consolidating your debt with a personal loan to eliminate the monthly high-interest payments.

Home repairs, appliance replacements, air conditioner replacement, and auto repairs will often exceed our savings, especially if you are young and just starting out in your career. When these large expenses become necessary, it is always fruitful to evaluate your financing options. The difference in interest rates between charging the expenses on a credit card, getting a bank loan, or financing them through an independent contractor can make a major difference in the monthly payment for these debts.

Let's look at the differences between financing a $10,000 home repair bill to be paid off in four years—forty-eight months—through a credit card versus a loan. Credit card interest can run as high as 32 percent, but for our purposes we will say it's 20 percent, which is closer to the average. The interest rate on a bank loan can also vary a lot, but the average is around 8 percent.

	Credit Card	Bank Loan
Interest Rate	20%	8%
Initial amount borrowed	$10,000	$10,000
Payments	$304.30/month	$244.13/month
Total paid in 48 months:	$14,606.40	$11,718.20

Anyone who needs to finance a loan like this will find that the $60 per month savings will make a substantial difference during the four-year payoff period.

Being a Lender

You become a lender when you are paid for saving—when the level of your savings account gets beyond what you expect to need for emergencies, you can consider CDs, bonds, or bond funds. CDs are a great option because they are safe investments that offer a higher interest rate than most savings accounts, but there is a penalty for accessing the funds before maturity. Bonds, on the other hand, are longer-term investments that offer greater returns and a predictable income, but can expose you to some risks. Bond funds are mutual funds that hold a portfolio of bonds at a lower-cost access. While you are invested in accounts such as these, you should reinvest the interest whenever you can, as any reinvested interest increases your net worth. Whether savings accounts are paying 1 or 6 percent, every month in which you accumulate interest that you do not spend increases your net worth and, therefore, your future standard of living.

In all cases, if you are lending, the quality of the loan determines not only how likely you are to be paid back in a timely manner but also the time you will have to spend servicing the debt. At the time of this writing, credit cards were charging 14 to 30 percent interest, online and personal loans charged 10 to 35 percent, while payday loans—a short-term, high-cost loan to cover immediate financial needs that is typically due on your next payday—charged 390 to 600 percent interest. But if you choose to be a payday lender, you will be spending a lot of time chasing people for repayments and repossessing items put up as collateral. Most lenders will choose not to be in the loan-servicing business and will instead choose the lower rates with no servicing requirements—savings accounts, CDs, bonds, bond funds, and ETFs. All of these are compared to U.S. government paper, a risk-free investment that is backed by the government and yields 2 to 4.5 percent.

When we lend money by making deposits in a savings account or purchasing CDs and bonds, we know within reason what our investment is worth. A bank savings account or short-term CD will be worth near the deposited amount while accounts at brokerage firms will price CDs and bonds near their market value, and the agent can shop those securities for the best prices if you choose to liquidate them before the maturity date. The entire principal is repaid upon the maturity date. Interest is normally paid either every six months or in total at maturity.

Maturity Terms, Long-Term
Interest Rates, and Bond Prices

Avoiding unnecessary risks is key to properly investing funds and collecting interest. In the 1970s, when interest rates on U.S. Treasuries went above 15 percent, there were some issues with 30-year Treasury bonds going to 50 cents on the dollar. Here were some of the safest securities in the world, selling at half price. The lesson here is that you should not be foolish when looking at the terms of a loan. When you buy U.S. Treasury bonds, you are lending to the United States government. If five-year rates are at 2 percent and thirty-year rates are at 4, then there is a temptation to go for double the yield on these "safe" instruments. However, if rates go to 12 percent on a thirty-year $1000 bond, the bond price would go down to $354. Let's take a serious look at these numbers.

TREASURY BONDS		
Term	5-Year	30-Year
Principal	$1,000	$1,000
Interest	2%	12%
Price	$1,000	$354

This is an extreme example of the risk, but it's a good illustration of why you shouldn't look at longer terms when lending money. In contrast to equity investments, which should always be approached with a long-term outlook, investors should look to the shorter term when lending money at interest, and all loans, CDs, and bond purchases should be approached with the probability of owning the investment until maturity. It is true that they can be liquidated early in almost all cases, but that alternative should not be part of the evaluation process.

An exception to the practice of lending at interest for a shorter term would be for an investor to put a calculated portion of bond money into long-term treasuries, AAA-rated corporates, or related ETFs when the rates are exceedingly high—10 percent or more—but we have yet to see those higher rates in this century.

The charts below illustrate how bond prices can change when rates change—and these changes will be more extreme on the longer-term issues. The first chart is the price of the Treasury Long-Term (TLT), an ETF managed by BlackRock. These ETFs were created at the turn of the century, and the periods in the second chart on TLT and SHY, another ETF managed by BlackRock, start in 2003 and run into 2024. This was a period when long-term Treasury rates went down from 5.3 to 1.25 percent. The TLT chart shows that an investment in the portfolio would have fluctuated between a high of $165 and a low of $84. That is quite a swing—even in a period when the rates were only as high as 5.3 percent. These long-term rates have been as high as 15.8 percent.

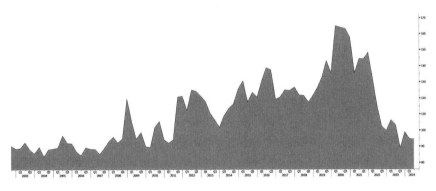

The price of the TLT (iShares 20+ Treasury bond ETF) 2000–2024.
Courtesy of Bloomberg L.P.

The second chart shows that short-term Treasury prices ranged between $79.10 and $86.60 during this period. This ETF is a portfolio of 1- to 3-year Treasury bonds, and the chart illustrates how shorter-term bonds fluctuate much less and therefore expose the investor to much less risk.

Note that we are using ETF charts here as illustrations. Smaller investors will find funds, mutual funds, and ETFs more efficient due to their lower investment minimums and limited risk, while larger investors will have more success with bonds because they are more expensive but offer a more stable income. A round lot (or the standard minimum trading size) in bonds is $25,000, and many bond quotes from inventory desks will limit offerings to minimum purchases of that amount.

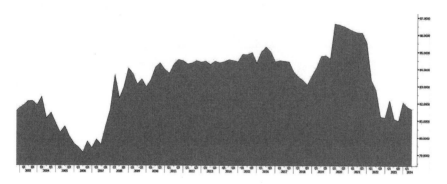

The price of SHY, an EFT managed by BlackRock, showing short-term Treasury prices. Courtesy of Bloomberg L.P.

The last chart shows the rate on the ten-year Treasury, a much-used middle-maturity Treasury bond that has seen rates as low as 0.66% and as high as 15.8%. Note that this chart goes all the way back to 1962. No financial expert knows how interest rates will fluctuate, yet your job as an investor is to collect interest with the safe portion of your portfolio, or the percentage that is allocated to low-risk, income-generating investments. If you overinvest when rates are low, you may end up locking your money for the duration of the security, because the price will fall rapidly when interest rates rise. If you tie up assets in long-term maturities, you are taking a risk that rates will go higher and prices will go lower, precluding the use of your money for any other attractive opportunities that may arise.

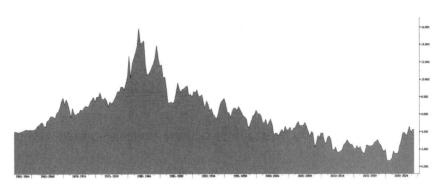

Price of the ten-year Treasury over time. Courtesy of Bloomberg L.P.

The bottom line is this: you must always beware of the length of the instrument, whether you are lending or borrowing.

Careful Lending—Loans to Friends or Relatives

Any kind of loan is a business transaction, even if you are lending money to a family member or friend. The absolute first consideration is how this transaction might affect your long-term investment plans. While making a loan like this is a family matter, it should always be evaluated in light of how the transaction will affect your own lifestyle, investments, and future. As we saw in chapter 4, the sad fact is that there is only a fifty-fifty chance that your relative will ever repay you.

There is a very real risk that you will never see the money you lend to a family member again, and you should not assume that risk unless you determine that its loss would not have a significant effect on your own financial situation. If you do make that determination, you need to be aware that the IRS requires all loans, to family members or otherwise, be at or near market interest rate levels. Any difference between the going interest rate and what you charge on a personal loan to a family member will be considered a gift by the IRS and is subject to taxes. Any loan forgiveness is also considered a gift. Small loans that involve only small amounts of interest are of little consequence, but anything above the annual tax-free gift level—which is $17,000 at the time of this writing—can significantly impact both your finances as well as those of the recipient. Yet it is also important to note that this limit is on an individual level, so a couple can gift $34,000 per year to an individual or even $68,000 to another couple. If you are contemplating any transaction approaching or exceeding these limits, you should involve an accountant to make sure it complies with tax laws.

Chapter 6

Illiquid Investments

B efore we discuss illiquid investments, let's consider our definition of liquidity. Liquidity refers to the investor's ability to easily convert an asset into liquid cash without affecting its market price. In looking at two Dow Jones stocks at random, Microsoft and ExxonMobil, the spread between the bid and the asked price almost never exceeds ten cents. At a price of $300 for Microsoft and $110 for Exxon, those spreads were less than one-tenth of a percent on ExxonMobil stock, and less than one-twenty-fifth on Microsoft. That means that there is virtually no difference in the buying and selling price of those stocks—this is real liquidity.

The U.S. Dollar is the supreme example of ultimate liquidity. We are fortunate to live in a country that has the most stable currency in the world—if you have ten hundred-dollar bills, you can get credit for a $1000 deposit or exchange those hundreds for tens, twenties, or fifties at your bank. This is the ultimate liquidity.

When you measure your net worth, you need to use the bid value of your assets. That means taking the published value of those assets and using them to calculate your total. If you own stocks, bonds, or funds, you can use the published values on those investments, but if you own illiquid investments, it can be very difficult to value them. You must also prepare for greater fluctuations in value for these assets over economic cycles.

There are many types of illiquid investments, from baseball cards, rare coins, documents and mineral rights, to toys. One of my clients made money collecting and trading G.I. Joe relics. Many people have collections of Legos, Star Wars, or Avatar toys. Collectibles like these should be considered hobbies, however, because there is a big spread between what you might pay for one of these items and what it can be sold for. Experienced collectors can make money collecting and trading these items, but they are collections, not investments.

When evaluating the liquidity of wealth, we must look at the spread between the current wholesale price and the retail price. If I buy something this morning, what is the bid if I choose to sell it before noon? If there is no visible bid, then there is a lack of liquidity. I am not going to tell you to never own illiquid investments, but for the purposes of long-term planning you should understand the difference between liquid and illiquid assets.

Private Offerings

Private investments can range from an investment that is not traded on a stock exchange to one that does not have a daily price listing.

Any formal offerings of a private investment must be registered with the SEC and provide a prospectus, or a brochure containing information on the nature of the business—primarily the breakdown of shares being offered, the current ownership, the debt of the company, and other relevant information. An investor planning to put money into a private offering of this nature should carefully read and study the offering prospectus, as it will sometimes differ from the verbal pitch that they received from the salesperson raising money for the company.

In any case where you are putting money into a private offering, you should plan to be without the invested money for at least several months.

More often than not, investors in this type of venture will be asked to add to their investment. New companies usually raise money several times before the business begins to provide an income to the investors.

Real Estate

Many, many fortunes have been made from real estate investments, yet it is a relatively illiquid investment, depending on the type of real estate investment you hold.

For example, raw land is a more illiquid investment than income-producing property. An apartment complex, a house, a warehouse, or any other leasable property can be valued by the income it produces or is expected to produce. A real estate professional can easily show the income stream and give a good estimate of the annual expenses, insurance, taxes, and maintenance that the property will likely require. From those numbers an investor can make an educated decision on the investment value.

A plot of raw land, however, is a different story. We've all seen plots of land in very busy areas go unsold and undeveloped for decades. There can be any number of reasons why these plots aren't developed, even if there are good annual returns on their values. Some reasons that properties go unsold include disputed titles, missing heirs, zoning restrictions, zoning disputes, and long-term traffic route problems. But, whether we know why a particular plot of land goes unsold or not, it is undisputed that there are no daily quotes on these investments and their value will vary greatly over time depending upon numerous factors—including the zoning of the property, the resolution of its estate, and the fluctuating interests of developers in the area. Any investment in raw land should be made with the understanding that the money could be tied up for a long, long time, even if the investment ultimately proves to be very profitable.

Investments in income-producing properties provide a bit more liquidity. Some investors buy those properties to dress them up and resell at a higher price. Others invest in properties for a longer term with the intent to benefit from the income stream they produce. In either case, the investor should be aware that their money could be tied up for many months, especially when the market changes unexpectedly. When the Federal Reserve begins raising rates rapidly, the real estate markets can freeze up quickly. If you are caught with a large inventory of property and forced to sell, the price could be much, much lower than you had expected.

Gold

Centuries ago, family wealth was measured primarily by how much gold bullion or gold coins they had stored away. Gold was considered the standard of wealth and was somewhat liquid, especially in good economic times. That standard of wealth is somewhat diminished today, but there is still a quoted value on gold, and it is somewhat liquid. However, in the last forty years, gold has failed to keep up with inflation and has severely lagged in the stock markets.

If you buy a gold coin at the local precious metals store, you will pay anywhere between a 40 to 80 percent markup from the dealer's cost. If you have enough money to buy larger quantities of gold coins off an exchange, the markup shrinks to about 20 percent. Gold bullion comes in larger quantities, and the margins are a bit smaller. In all cases, if you invest in gold, you will pay someone a very nice markup. Anything with a large markup between the wholesale and the retail price is not considered a liquid investment.

As Warren Buffet said, gold is nothing more than a mineral that "gets dug out of the ground in Africa, or someplace. Then we melt it down, dig another hole, bury it again, and pay people to stand around guarding it. It has no utility. Anyone watching from Mars would be scratching their head."

We get bombarded with ads telling us to buy gold as insurance against war, famine, inflation, and many other calamities. However, it has not offered very much protection in recent decades, and the long-term liquidity of gold is somewhat in question.

Gold first hit $800 per ounce in 1980. The midpoint price that year was about $550 per ounce. At the time of this writing, the price of gold is in the low $1,800s. That's about a 3 percent rate of increase per year, which is somewhere close to the inflation rate over that same period of time. Yet the Dow Jones Industrial Average has gone from 3,400 to over 32,000, which is over an 8 percent rate of return. And during that time, we had the Cold War and five bear markets, including the Great Recession and the banking collapse of 2007–2008, as well as several periods of economic uncertainty. Gold has proven to be a highly variable store of wealth, and a very unreliable hedge against inflation. The most important statistic with reference to gold in the whole period from 1980 to 2023 is that dividend payouts, actual cash payouts, were greater than the average increase in the price of gold. And the increase in the price of the Dow, which does not include dividends, was almost a ten-to-one ratio. And if I had needed to sell my Dow Jones stocks during that period, I could have sold them at any working hour of any day.

There have been periods of time when gold was the default alternative to collapsing currencies. People fleeing the German-controlled countries during World War II sought gold coins and bullion to preserve wealth during relocation. And two decades before that, after the end of World War I in 1918, when the German Mark began to collapse (by November of 1923, one U.S. Dollar was equal to $4.2 trillion marks), gold and silver had become stores of wealth for those who could get their hands on them.[1]

In 1933, President Roosevelt persuaded congress to officially detach the U.S. Dollar from the price of gold. However, the dollar was still unofficially priced in terms of gold because the dollar was, presumably, convertible into gold. It was President Nixon who "closed the gold window" and ended the privilege of converting dollars to gold. The liquidity of gold was officially over.

Diamonds

Diamonds may sparkle, but their investment value usually lags the S&P stock index and rarely keeps up with the Consumer Price Index (CPI). And even the largest, most valuable of diamonds will never pay you a dividend.

The strongest argument against using diamonds to store wealth is the difference between the bidding and asking prices. If you really want to see the spread in these values, just borrow a nice diamond from one of the ladies in your family and go get a bid on it from a diamond dealer. Then go to a jewelry store, find a similar stone, and check the price. You will normally find a 50 to 100 percent differential in those prices—and those prices have suffered severely during depressed economic times. These traits keep diamonds from being a truly liquid investment.

Uninsured Deposits

The Federal Reserve Bank often creates a low-interest-rate environment to stimulate the economy. This practice usually helps the economy, but is a penalty to those who have depended on interest from savings to augment their income. During these times, offshore banks often advertise higher interest rates, and many people will move their money to banks in the Cayman Islands and other foreign countries. After all, when CD rates are running at 3 percent in the United States and an island bank is offering 6, the temptation to invest some or all of your money with that bank is very strong. It is a bank and, considering everything, banks are generally a safe place to put your money, right?

All we have to do to overcome that temptation is consider how many of those banks failed during the last recessions—and remember that there is no FDIC insurance on deposits in offshore accounts. In general, those deposits are uninsured deposits. This means that if the bank fails, all the money is gone.

During my career as an assets manager, I was responsible for many accounts in the Mexican resort towns for citizens of the United States and Canada who had retired in those areas. No matter how often I warned against uninsured deposits, countless people lost a great portion or all of their money when these banks failed. Many of these sad cases came to light in the Mexico resort areas of Chapala, Ajijic, San Miguel de Allende, and Mazatlán. The advertising was really good, but the failures came during every economic cycle.

Many developed countries, including the United States and the European Union, have insurance for bank deposits up to certain levels. In the U.S., that limit is currently $250,000 per account per category at each bank. Any couple can have multiple category accounts—for example, a husband and wife can each have a separate account, they can have a joint account together, and then they can each have their own IRA account. Once those limits are reached, additional accounts can be opened at another bank with a separate insurance coverage. In contrast, investing in CDs at banks that have no insurance can be very risky, as it is almost impossible to get the financials of a bank that sells uninsured CDs.

Corporations face the problem of needing to maintain very large bank deposits in order to operate their daily business. One of the key jobs of a chief financial officer (CFO) is to keep up with the status of the bank in which the company stores its daily cash balances. If the bank fails, the company loses all the money in the bank above the $250,000 insured limit. Bank failures loom large in times of financial crisis.

Annuities

I will be careful not to offend those who sell annuities and those who own them. The annuity is a highly advertised, widely owned insurance product, and it is an appropriate investment for many households and corporations. I, myself, was personally licensed to sell and did sell annuities for over forty years as part of my team's advisory business. Annuities can be very useful in corporate retirements, 401(k)s, structured settlements, lottery payouts, and many other applications. But my purpose in this chapter is to distinguish liquid from illiquid assets, and so here I must define the limitations of this financial arrangement.

First and foremost, the annuity is an insurance policy. Our team resource for annuities defined it as "a contract with an insurance company—not an investment." Terms and returns on annuities can vary widely, and one term that you absolutely must evaluate is the internal rate of return. If you own a 3-percent one-year CD and the interest is paid at the end of the year, the internal rate of return is 3 percent. If the interest is paid twice a year, the return goes up slightly due to internal compounding—by 0.0225, making the internal rate of return 3.0225 percent. If you own a one-year, three-year, five-year, or ten-year annuity, you are guaranteed that 3 percent return for the period of the contract, and it is insured by the insurance company offering the annuity. The period and the maturity are guaranteed, too, but you should know the terms of an early cash-out. If you buy a ten-year fixed annuity, the salesman will likely get a 6 percent commission and the early cash-out penalty will start at around 8 percent, eventually declining to zero or near zero. If the annuity is fixed, you don't need to worry too much about the internal costs, only the net return and cash-out rate.

However, the terms of variable annuities can vary greatly, and the administrative and management fees will likely be 1 to 2 percent each year. Buying an annuity can also be an expensive process, especially when you compare it with an investment account. Account management fees on Registered Investment Advisor (RIA) accounts can run as low as 0.5 percent per year.

The good thing about annuities, however, is that the insurance company accepts the risk and guarantees the net fixed rate over and above the internal cost. Most states additionally have a further guarantee that protects the annuity owner in case something happens to the insurance company.

But the title of this chapter is "Illiquid Investments."

I recently looked at the posted rates for annuities from several insurance companies and saw that rates were running from 4.4 to 5 percent for five-year fixed-rate annuities. Those rates compared favorably with five-year CD rates at the time and exceeded those on the five- and ten-year Treasury bonds. However, the typical surrender rates, or the penalty for taking money from an annuity before it matures, started at 8 percent the first year, and declined only to 4 percent in the fifth year. These high surrender charges do not make this an illiquid investment, but they do impose a high penalty for cashing in early—and the five-year fixed annuity is one of the most liquid. Once you annuitize a sum of money for life with an insurance company, that sum should be considered gone—only the periodic payments are certain. There are secondary markets for life annuities where other buyers will offer to buy the income stream, but the seller must take a big loss in order to make that sale.

Variable-index annuities attract a lot of attention. The advertising message is that you can enjoy the upside of an annuity without ever experiencing the downside. Contract specifications will give the investor a portion of the upside in the stock market while still protecting the owner against loss. But before you buy this type of annuity, there are a number of questions you should ask: What is the annual fee on the contract? What are the fees on the equity funds inside this contract? What is the limit on my growth potential? What are the cash-out fees, and is there a declining schedule in those fees? Many variable annuities will limit growth in any given year to 6 percent. If you avoid a big loss with a downside guarantee, you may be happy enough with the 6 percent upside, but in a year when the market is up 20 percent or more this limit can be very disappointing. You should always review the nature of the contract carefully and make sure you understand it before you purchase this—or any—kind of annuity.

I recall one client, a retired doctor, who insisted on buying a life-with-ten-year-certain annuity or straight-life annuity (both types of annuities that guarantee income for life) any time he freed up some money—from accumulations of cash and maturities of bonds to IRA distributions. I talked to him about diversifying his assets, but his objective was maximum current income, and so I sold him the annuities as requested. His current income was guaranteed by those insurance companies with the best rates at the time.

There is great confidence in having an insured income for life. Many corporations use annuities to guarantee the incomes of retiring workers. A company can buy an annuity, write off the expense, and depend upon the insurance company to make the monthly payments to the retiree. But there are costs for those guarantees, and the buyer should evaluate them before making the purchase.

Art

Most of the art investors I've met have been long-term oriented, and the short-term fluctuations have not been as dramatic as in other forms of relatively illiquid investments. It may be more expensive to buy a painting by Van Gogh, Monet, or da Vinci than it is to invest in diamonds or gold, but it's actually safter in the long-term. Paying up for a painting by a supposedly up-and-coming artist, however, is much more of a gamble.

Picking good art is quite a risk for anyone without experience. My wife Kay and I were strolling through art renderings along the Grand Canal on a vacation trip to Venice once when we spotted a nice original work of art depicting Marco Polo's house. We picked up the painting for about $300, not because we considered it a good investment but because we liked it. Upon our return stroll along the same street, we saw the artist with a marked-up canvas, painting a brand-new yet identical work. We had no illusions about the uniqueness of the painting or the artist.

Later, in the hotel, we saw a lady reveling about buying an "original" painting that she and her family would cherish as a good investment—it was the same painting. Her opinion may have been that it was a good investment, but we considered it simply a good piece of art for the dining room. I have not seen, nor do I expect to see, that artist's name again.

Investments in art should be very long-term in nature. Art collection is a hobby just like any sport—running, tennis, or pickleball. A few people are good enough to earn money playing tennis, but the great majority of people do it because we enjoy the game. That same principle holds in the art world—a few investors can make money appraising and buying artworks, while the rest of us just appreciate good art.

Structured Settlements and Life Settlements

A structured settlement is a payout of a settlement obligation, normally from the settlement of a lawsuit, over time. These payouts are almost always made through an annuity. A life settlement, on the other hand, is the purchase of a payout on someone's life, usually from a life insurance policy. The seller of the life insurance policy gives up ownership to the buyer in the death benefit. While a structured settlement is paid out over specific period of time, a life settlement can have unspecified terms, because life contracts depend upon the unscheduled death of the person covered by the original policy. In both cases, the original contracts normally involve high-rated insurance companies that can be expected to make the payments through good times and bad, though they are considered illiquid investments.

A buyer of these income streams will undertake varying risks, depending upon the terms of purchase. If the purchase involves a direct payment from a healthy insurance company, the default risks are minimal. Most legitimate insurance companies, which are subject to a lot of regulations, are safe, but buying from resellers means taking on risks that will vary widely, as does the liquidity of these investments. If you invest in the payment stream rather than in the policy, the risks are increased. Your investment will be subject to the balance sheet of the repurchasing company, and the investment becomes even more illiquid.

If you are looking to invest in settlements such as these, it is important that you know how many commissions and expense streams come out of the investment before the ultimate buyer receives the payments. Before making any investments, you should get advice from an unbiased and independent advisor.

Slogans and Quotes

I will now share some of the more well-known slogans in the investment world. These sayings have been used regularly by professionals in this world, and they all portray elements of good investment practices.

"Buy the rumor, sell the news."

Very few total surprises hit the stock markets. If oil inventories are about to show a serious decline, the price of crude oil will most often be up before the news officially breaks. The government agencies responsible for reporting these things are sworn to secrecy, but somehow enough investors get a whiff of the news ahead beforehand that there is often a peak before the official news release. This same scenario is played out in interest-rate changes by the Fed, all kinds of commodity prices, mergers, and corporate earnings releases. Short-term investing is near gambling, and buying or selling on press releases is sheer folly.

In the year 1999, there was a worldwide panic over the century changeover, and many folks were convinced something ominous was coming—the end of civilization, international computer meltdowns, and changes in the earth's rotation and calendar as we knew it. Media companies all over the world jumped on the story, and the subject engulfed a lot of conversations. The year end was given the name Y2K, and a lot of headlines warned of dire possibilities. In every country, there were people who cashed out and sought shelter in the outback to avoid the coming chaos. Thousands of people would not sleep the night of the new year, and afterward, many refused to believe that nothing had changed except a larger number on the calendar—and a greater number of hangovers. The stock market was actually up the first trading day of the new millennium.

It proved to be an extreme case of betting on the news.

"The market will do what it must to surprise the greatest number of investors."

It is a source of frustration for many would-be traders, but the fact is that it is virtually impossible to predict from one day to the next what markets will do in the short run. The market could be way down today, and for no apparent reason shoot up again tomorrow. Or the news can be horrible, and the market will be up. It is another example of "buy on the rumor, sell on the news"—the hype is almost always greater than reality.

"In bear markets, shares return to their rightful owners."

This saying is widely credited to J. P. Morgan, but many prominent asset managers have quoted this slogan as well, including Warren Buffett. I have previously warned against the stupid—and very common—practice of selling good stocks in a bear market. You never know how long or how deep a market decline will be.

An equity investor must be willing to hold on to good equities through a decline.

"There are old traders, and there are bold traders, but there are no old, bold traders."

Throughout the brokerage industry and in most large investment advisory firms there are "trading desks" or "trading departments." These units exist for the purpose of receiving orders and placing them on the proper exchanges or markets and then working to get the best price. Many of the operators of these desks are called "traders." Many corporations also have units where employees trade in the commodities that are used in their business—food companies will buy futures on food commodities, and oil companies will sell current production using futures on oil and gas. But these "traders" are not to be confused with the short-term investors who are also called "traders." An investment trader is someone who attempts to make money from short-term swings in stocks, commodities, or derivatives.

There are many stories of people who have made and lost fortunes as traders, yet there are only a few who have been successful in the long term.

Probably the best-known trader in the markets was Jesse Livermore. He made over $100 million in his career—more than $1.5 billion in today's dollars—but he went broke multiple times. He made multiple fortunes by trading, but he lost it all and filed for bankruptcy in 1908. After recovering his losses, he went bankrupt again in 1915. Then, after making huge amounts of money with short stocks during the 1929 market collapse, he filed for bankruptcy once more in 1934. Livermore still worked at various positions on Wall Street after that, but he shot himself in a Manhattan hotel room on November 28, 1940. He left a note to his wife at the time, whom he called Nina, saying, "I am a failure. I am truly sorry but this is the only way out for me."[1]

"Fantasy is more exciting than reality."

This slogan highlights the tendency to trade on the strength of a rumor. Over the years, we have all heard many rumors highlighting miracle opportunities from one development or another, miracle cures for cancer that never panned out, or discoveries of massive diamond or gold deposits. It can be really tempting to buy into some fantasy. Yet almost all of the fantasies we hear about are actually less exciting in reality, and very, very few offer good short-term investment opportunities.

"Formula for success: rise early, work hard, strike oil."
—J. Paul Getty

Of course Mr. Getty was joking when he said this, but he was also acknowledging that extreme wealth tends to be the result of both good management and luck—being in the right place, with the right tools, at the right time. For example, Warren Buffet is often called the Oracle of Omaha. He can claim many successes in his investment history, but much of his wealth is due to good fortune as well. He gives credit to his serendipity in being hired by Ben Graham, a very successful investment manager at that time, attributes his success to his being able to double his portfolio values in the first three years as an investment manager, and to meeting with Charlie Munger and becoming his business partner. Extreme wealth is almost always developed by those who are responsible with money but have also been alert and responsive at the right time.

"It is not how much money you make, but how much money you keep, how hard it works for you, and how many generations you keep it for." —Robert Kiyosaki

Mr. Kiyosaki made his money in and has written a lot about real estate, which is very different from the securities markets. However, many of his messages apply to other kinds of investing. Many fortunes have been made by people who have spent all their earnings. High-income earners get a lot of attention for their success, but ultimate success should be measured by what those people do with their earnings. Be responsible with the money you make, keep your expenses well below your income, don't borrow foolishly, and be conscious of the estate you are building for yourself and your heirs.

"Financial peace isn't the acquisition of stuff. It's learning to live on less than you make, so you can give money back and have money to invest. You can't win until you do this." —Dave Ramsey

Living on less than you make may be the hardest to follow of all the recommendations you get from successful people. When you're at the bottom of the earnings ladder and there are certain things society demands of you, it can be hard to save money. Getting enough education for yourself and your kids is paramount, as is providing a safe and stable home environment. However, the tendency is to overestimate the level of expense that is necessary, even in this truly essential category. For example, you can work while taking classes, or your kids can live at home and work while attending a community college.

"In investing, what is comfortable is rarely profitable." —Robert Arnott

Once again, we are reminded that investing is not a short-term process. It would be much more comfortable to invest today and profit tomorrow—or at least to know what your investment will be worth tomorrow. It is uncomfortable to put money to work today and know that you do not intend to touch it for many, many months.

During one decline in the 1970s, ExxonMobil traded with a dividend yield of 10 percent. One of my clients bought one thousand shares, saying that he wasn't concerned with how low it might go. Almost forty years later, ExxonMobil traded at a 10 percent dividend yield yet again, and I bought the stock for several clients. It was extremely uncomfortable to buy anything at either time because markets were severely depressed, but those were both near-low prices for ExxonMobil, and it paid off in the long run.

"Know what you own and why you own it." —Peter Lynch

Peter Lynch was a longtime successful portfolio manager for Fidelity Funds, and for many years he managed the Magellan Fund, which became one of the largest funds in the world. Lynch said that his long-term average success rate while making investments was about 60 percent. That number might be somewhat lower than you think it should be when it comes to investing, but the reality is that most of the capital gains in any portfolio come from just 60 percent of the investments, even in a good list of stocks. Lynch did not buy dogs in the other 40 percent of his portfolios—the other 40 percent also had to do reasonably well for the entire list to be competitive. If you're right in 60 percent of your investments and responsible in the other 40, the long-term results can be quite rewarding.

"Investing should be more like watching paint dry or watching grass grow. If you want excitement, take $800 and go to Las Vegas." —Paul Samuelson

I have repeatedly stressed the importance of looking to the long term when it comes to your investments. While this quote was originally said when $800 was worth much more than it is today, it demonstrates the importance of taking gambling out of the investment process. Investing should not be a party or some other extravagant venture—it is a slow and painstaking way to grow your hard-earned savings, bit by bit.

"Don't look for the needle in the haystack. Just buy the haystack!" —John Bogle

Many times in this book I have recommended diversifying your holdings to reduce risk. This quote by John Bogle sums it up nicely—your job as an investor is not to find the absolute best investment in the myriad of available opportunities, but to own good groups of investments so that you can absorb any losses.

"An investment in knowledge pays the best interest." —Benjamin Franklin

This quote emphasizes the value of educating yourself on good investment practices by taking advantage of the investments in knowledge made by others. The more knowledge there is backing your professional investment advice, the more valuable that advice will be.

"Invest today for a secure tomorrow."

Most of these quotes and slogans are summaries of general prin-ciples, not detailed pieces of advice. All we need to understand the wisdom of this principle is to look at the alternative—not investing today will likely lead to an insecure tomorrow. Many, many books have been written on detailed strategies for investing wisely, and the process can seem daunting. But you should not let those details or the sheer volume of information deter you from investing your money. You must invest today to have money for tomorrow.

"Do not regret getting in late or getting out too early."

Most of the information that you find out about companies will become available only after the stocks or the markets begin to move. Trying to be ahead of news announcements is futile—your real job is to absorb the new information and assess whether the announcement has changed the long-term perspective on the value of your investment. A surprise dip in the sales of a single product by a large multiline company may be a one-off event. A move by the Federal Reserve to change interest rates, on the other hand, may affect business for many months to come.

"Investing never goes out of fashion."

We can go all the way back to biblical times and find stories about investing in vineyards, orchards, and herds of animals, among other things. Without those commodities producing consumer goods, there would be no investments—and no people. The investing process has been refined over many centuries, and will hopefully continue to be refined in the centuries to come. But in one form or another, investing in the production of products necessary for civilization has stayed in fashion throughout the ages—fortunately.

"Financial intelligence pays off."

It is not the job of the individual investor to know everything about stocks, bonds, and markets. A good investment firm or advisor will have access to financial intelligence that you as an individual investor are not privy to and will therefore be able to better advise your investments. Your risk comes if you ignore good intelligence.

"The most dangerous words in investing are 'it's different this time.'" —Sir John Templeton

John Templeton was a portfolio manager for many decades with a very successful record, and he founded the Templeton group of funds. The Templeton group became very large, and they have been used widely with a successful track record for many decades until they were purchased by Franklin Funds in 1992. His company operated out of the Bahamas, but the funds he managed were widely used in the United States, and he spent much of his time here.

Every market decline brings out the doomsayers telling us why things are different this time. We know that all cycles have unique variables, but we have seen the economy recover from every inflation spike, every interest rate high, every war, and every economic downturn. We have records going back to Europe, well before Columbus discovered America. These records show us how the recoveries played out—and how business resumed.

"Those who cannot remember the past are condemned to repeat it." —George Santayana

This quote from George Santayana resembles another slogan that is frequently repeated in investment circles: "History repeats itself, which is good because most people don't pay attention the first time." The author of this one is not defined, but it highlights the traits of market declines and recoveries—if we do not learn from past mistakes, we are doomed to repeat them again and again.

"If there is one common theme to the vast range of crises . . . It is that excessive debt accumulation, whether it be by the government, banks, corporations, or consumers, often poses more systemic risks than it seems during a boom." —Carmen Reinhart

I have warned against debt several times already in this book—but it is still not enough. Debt causes a huge amount of grief for everyone involved, whether it be on an individual or national level. As I mentioned in chapter 4, a 2022 study by the U.S. Consumer Financial Protection Bureau about borrowers who used BNPL—that is, Buy Now Pay Later—reported that 62 percent of them also used credit cards for major purchases, in comparison to only 44 percent of those who did not use BNPL.[2] That is just one more illustration of how addictive buying on a margin can become.

The financial crisis of 2007–2008 was caused primarily by the surfacing of obscure debts from around the world. At the time, there were over $60 trillion in obligations through credit default swaps, a derivative method of trading debt obligations, and that number had ballooned from $13 trillion in just four years. These credit default swaps could be purchased in huge amounts on debts, currencies, bonds, mortgages, and interest rate changes. Because profits were also huge, financial firms, banks, insurance companies, and other firms began issuing these instruments. When the economy reversed, liabilities occurred and bankruptcies became rampant. Defaults began to appear in all countries.

In 2007, the average reserves of U.S. banks were only 1.7 percent, meaning that many banks had exposures of sixty times their equity reserves. After the crisis, the developed nations began requiring bank reserves to be 10 percent or greater.

"You get recessions, you have stock market declines. If you don't understand that's going to happen, then you're not ready. You won't do well in the markets." —Peter Lynch

It is always a shock to see how many new investors are surprised, even astonished, when a recession occurs or the stock market declines. Throughout this book, I have advised you to invest your money for the long term in good, profitable businesses. Every business, every economy, and every stock market will have periods of decline. That is why you put your savings in a liquid, stable account but treat your investments as long-, long-term projects.

"I don't look for seven-foot bars. I look for one-foot bars that I can step over." —Warren Buffett

My interpretation of this quote is that investing is not rocket science or brain surgery. The math and the processes are usually quite simple and should not be viewed as too complicated. Investing should be a simple and happy experience.

"I will tell you how to become rich. Close the door. Be fearful when others are greedy. Be greedy when others are fearful." —Warren Buffett

This is another piece of advice telling you not to get caught up in market fluctuations. A stock that fluctuates between $8 and $10 may actually be a good investment in the long run, especially if it pays a good dividend. However, if you can buy the stock at $8 when others are "fearful," you will have a couple extra years of good returns on your investment.

"If you're gonna do dumb things because your stock goes down, you shouldn't own the stock at all." —Warren Buffett

Buffett gets quoted a lot because he makes simple statements that sum up great insights about investing. This is just another quote reminding you that to succeed as an investor you need to look beyond the fluctuations of the stock market.

"The only reason to own a stock is its ultimate ability to pay me an income."

This slogan is often repeated by successful portfolio managers, and I include it here because it is key to making successful investments. All well-performing corporations will begin dividend payouts at some point, and those dividends will continue if the companies do well in the long run. For the past hundred years, dividends have produced over a third of the total return in the Dow Jones and S&P indexes.

"How many millionaires do you know who have become wealthy investing in savings accounts? I rest my case." —Robert G. Allen

A "savings account" is an account that holds emergency funds. Over the centuries, short-term deposits have averaged at 2 or 3 percent in interest, and inflation has run around 2 percent over the long term—just about the same as a savings account would yield. Business investments, on the other hand, have yielded an average of 8, 9, or 10 percent. Two-percent interest, not taking inflation into account, will double your money in about thirty-five years, but ten percent will double it in a fifth of that time.

"The market is filled with individuals who know the price of everything but the value of nothing." —Philip Fisher

A good analyst never cares much about the price of an investment. Most stock owners know the price of their holdings, but only the most attentive owners can give you a good estimate of their value. A stock's value is determined by a number of different factors, but the most important are knowing the price-to-earnings ratio, dividend rate, and any company trends. The price of Berkshire Hathaway has been above $400,000 per share without any worries from Warren Buffett, the company's CEO and one of the world's all-time leading investors.

At the other end of the price range, as we have seen, there are good reasons that the government and major firms have restrictions against buying stocks below $5.00 with borrowed money. But once we are above $5.00 per share, the price of any investment is much less important than the *value* of that investment.

"Buy some good stock and hold it till it goes up . . . If it don't go up, don't buy it." —Will Rogers

Will Rogers was being humorous when he explained the easy way to make money in the stock market. We all want to find stocks that go up, but it is unfortunately all too easy to find stocks that don't. In the late 1990s, I wrote an article for the local newspaper highlighting the prices of highly touted stocks in that era:

	1983 Price	1997 Price
ASA Ltd	37	33
Battle Mt. Gold	7	7
Bethlehem Steel	16	10
Cincinnati Milacron	24	24
Ethyl Corp	7	9
Homestake Mining	14	14
Humana Inc.	21	21
Kaufman & Broad	15	15
Skyline Homes	23	23
U.S. Steel	31	31
Winnebago	8	7

All of these were major companies at the time, but they are all examples of stocks that did not go up. And that was a period when the Dow Jones Industrial Average went from 1300 to 8100—a gain of 623 percent. The advice from Will Rogers to buy stocks that go up may sound good, but it's easier said than done. This is another good example of why you should diversify your investments, because you never know which ones will go up.

"The individual investor should act consistently as an investor and not as a speculator." —Benjamin Graham

Benjamin Graham, commonly acknowledged as the Father of Investing, wrote multiple books on investment practices and was a mentor to Warren Buffett. This quote is another reminder to take speculating out of your investing process and look to the long term.

I previously quoted another favorite slogan of Ben Graham's: "You can't time the market." This quote, alongside two of my other favorites, "Don't think it's easy to beat the market" and "Base your expectations not on optimism but on arithmetic," demonstrates the unpredictability of investing. The long-term averages on stocks and bonds round off at a nice 10 percent for the former and 5 for the latter. The best asset managers will beat those averages by a little bit over the long term, but not by much.

"Sort your money out." —Glen James

What does it mean to "sort your money out?" When you look at your money, you have pocket change, which can be a rattling nuisance. You have folding money, which can be the cash for purchases today. Then there's your bank accounts, which should always be enough to cover the checks you write. You have your savings accounts, which should be for emergencies only. And then you have your money for investments. It's easy to make the mistake of looking at all your money as one pot of cash without considering how it should be divided up, but you should be constantly evaluating the best way to sort your money.

"Invest today, enjoy tomorrow."

When we are investing for tomorrow, we mean the long-term future, not today or even the day after today. Any stock that pays a reliable dividend or any good-rated bond with a market interest rate provides the investor with income. The only reason to buy a stock is to ultimately receive an income, and adding any good stocks or bonds to your portfolio will increase your investments today and be a source of income tomorrow.

Comments on Often-Heard Quotes

South Coast Today ran an article by Jonathan Clements in April of 2001 titled "Excuses, excuses: how losers save face."[3] Below I have excerpted a few of the quotes, along with the translations of what they really mean:

- *"I'm happy to earn the market's return."* But only when stocks are going up.
- *"I have a very high risk tolerance."* I won't panic and sell until I've lost a truckload of money.
- *"I'm a conservative investor."* I have only half my portfolio in tech.
- *"I'm well diversified."* I own three stocks.
- *"I got this great stock tip."* My brother-in-law works out at this gym and there was this guy lifting weights, and he seemed really smart and he says . . .

Primer for Chapters 7–10

Being Responsible, Tending to Your Money, and Being Happy

As Warren Buffet said, "Unless you learn to make money while you sleep, you will have to work until you die." In this section, we will cover finding happiness while we work, caring for our assets, and doing the right things with our money to ensure our future prosperity.

Nothing in this book suggests that fast money is a reliable source of wealth. As Paul Getty advises us, "Rise early, work hard, and strike oil." We know that not everyone can invent the internet or strike oil, but we can practice good disciplines to increase our happiness.

Chapter 7

Caring for Your Assets

Personal discipline is the most important aspect of good investing. Yet just because an investor has achieved some success in building assets does not mean that they have mastered the art of being a disciplined person. Many investors who have achieved a measure of success will manage their own portfolios, and it is even more imperative that these investors maintain the discipline that I have been promoting throughout this book—adherence to the disciplines of good investing is critical. As I have stressed throughout this book, the wise investor is always searching for earnings and dividends. If you are managing your own investments, you should be buying stocks that show current success and a reasonable potential for future growth. The quest for fast money should take a back seat.

Sometimes it's easy to check into how companies are doing. Just like a good tire manager can tell you which tires are the best, a portfolio manager has the research to tell you which stocks to invest your hard-earned money in. One example of this kind of "research" from my own investing history occurred at our family breakfast table. The computer game Pac-Man by Namco had just become popular, and I was boasting about how I had sold the stock to many clients who had doubled or tripled their money in a very short time. My son Mitchell, who was a young junior high student at the time, said, "Well, you better get 'em out because nobody is doing that game anymore." I immediately went in to the office and began to sell the stock. The price of Atari eventually went from above $30 to under $1.

If you have achieved your goal of accumulating significant assets but are still managing your own investment portfolio, you should use all the resources available to you—such as research, industry news alerts, and account visibility—and avoid speculation in the process.

At the time of this writing, the general rule of thumb is that any assets under $500,000 are more efficient in funds, while assets above this threshold attract more alternatives, including management by a major asset manager. But the policies of investment houses vary—some firms preclude their advisors from accepting accounts less than $250,000, and others have a minimum of $500,000, $1 million, or more. Costs can be much higher on small managed accounts.

Successful investors are susceptible to the same risks that we all face in the investing process. Most successful investors have already weathered at least a few of these setbacks and have now arrived at the point where their biggest challenge is managing their assets.

To my readers whose assets now exceed a minimum investment amount, I want to stress that the proper investment strategies do not change: Your accounts should still be diversified. Your assets should be highly liquid. The primary safeguards should still be in place—avoid scams, don't transfer assets to third parties, refrain from putting money in stocks at the highs and taking it out at the lows, stay clear of gambling and short-term trading (especially in large amounts), avoid large transfers to family members or anyone you're in a romantic relationship with, and don't act out of greed.

Windfalls—Inherited, Earned, and Unearned

Just because someone achieves professional success or a great number of assets does not mean that person is immune to risk. Just because you received an inheritance, collected a big bonus, or won the lottery does not mean you can suddenly afford everything you have ever wanted. Even if you are given a great financial windfall, your spending habits should not change. As we saw in chapter 3, the sports and entertainment industry are filled with stories of successful people blowing their fortunes, and the same thing applies to those who inherit investible assets. It is easy to see new assets and decide that a nicer car, a bigger house, or a lake house should be in the picture. Before making any large purchases with your newly acquired assets, you should ask the following questions:

- Will my taxes be higher, and how do I plan for that?
- How will I invest these new assets?
- How much can I increase my spending without spending any of the new principal?
- What will my new income be?

All of these questions can be addressed with the help of a trusted tax advisor or portfolio manager.

Interest, Dividends, Rent, and Reinvestment

Most mistakes that new (and seasoned) investors make could be avoided if they asked a simple question: "What income will this investment pay me?"

As the slogan goes, "The only reason to own a stock is its ultimate ability to pay me an income." Growth is great—you want to invest in assets whose price will increase over the long term. But income is also important. As we have seen, profitable companies will pay out dividends to stockholders, and they will continue to pay out as long as they are doing well. Dividends account for more than one-third of the return in the performance of the Dow Jones and S&P 500 over the long haul. If instead of spending that income, you reinvest it, your wealth will accumulate more quickly.

Your income as an investor comes from the dividends paid out on stocks. You also receive interest on investments such as CDs. But other assets—real estate, for example—also pay income. My expertise is in financial securities rather than real estate, but let's look at an example.

What is the first decision that a real estate investor must make? An investor sees a property that is available for $1,000,000. That investor then searches for rents of comparable properties in the area and finds that they lease for around $100,000 per year. That sounds like a reasonable return on assets, but the seasoned investor will also consider insurance, maintenance, and taxes on the property. Assuming those costs are about $50,000 per year, the investor must consider whether a $50,000 net profit on the property is a reasonable return on the investment. If the investor borrows any money by using a mortgage, then the interest on that loan must also be taken into account. One hundred percent financing at 6 percent would throw the project into a net loss, because 6 percent of $1,000,000 is $60,000, versus the $50,000 cash flow on the $1,000,000 investment.

This is just one example, but a responsible investor must calculate what the cash flow will be for any investment. The stock of a company that is losing money and paying no dividend must be evaluated in terms of future cash flow and dividends. A portfolio or ETF averaging a P/E ratio of 20 and yielding only 1 percent is riskier than a portfolio trading at a 12 P/E and yielding 3 percent, because the former portfolio makes only five percent on the stock values while the latter makes 8.5—volatility increases with the price-to-earnings ratio.

Managing Your Investments:
Terms and Definitions

Investing is the same as any endeavor, in that there is a minimum amount of knowledge that you must have to do the job. While there is always a learning curve, it is important that you know the language and vocabulary to communicate with your investment advisor, CPA, and attorney.

Commodities

Everyone should know that an investor who is trading commodities is trading short-term and is gambling! As I pointed out in Chapter 4, if you buy a commodity contract, you are competing with the commodity desks at the major companies using those commodities in their business—if you buy an oil contract, you are competing with the professionals at Chevron and Exxon for a short-term profit with a leveraged contract, and buying a wheat contract puts you in competition with the commodity desks at General Mills and Kellanova. While the benefit of a commodity contract is that most require only about 10 percent of the money needed to purchase the good represented by that contract, there are significant risks associated with this type of trading. The typical investor is not schooled in the basics of any commodity and should not try to compete with the pros in the industry.

While long-term contracts are available, the great majority of commodity trading is less than one year in duration.

Options

While the average investor should never trade in commodities, diligent and responsible investors can *sometimes* use options. Stock options are a contract that grants the right to buy or sell a stock at a specific price and time, at which point it will expire. The most important thing to know is that about 66 percent of all options expire worthless, and we have seen periods where that number goes to 75 percent or more.

When dealing with options, the general principle is that option sellers make money, while option buyers lose money. The buyer of a "call" option, or a contract that grants the right to buy the stock in question, is paying a premium for making a bet that the stock will go up. The buyer of a "put" option, a contract that permits the stock's sale, is paying a premium for making a bet that the stock will go down. This is betting—and betting is gambling. Let me repeat that the responsible investor looks to the long term and avoids gambling in the short term.

The seller of a "covered call"—meaning that the underlying stock is owned in the portfolio—gets a premium for selling a stock at the "strike price," or the stated value at which the option is executed, while the seller of a "put" option receives a premium for buying a stock at the strike price. If the buyer has sufficient funds, selling "puts" can be a good way of acquiring a stock at a particular price.

Stock options are very complex, and they should only be used by professional investors or those few non-professional investors with a good understanding of them. In my many years of investment advising, I only knew a few investors I believed could confidently manage them.

Derivatives

Investment vehicles are numerous, but there are only two basic public securities—stocks and bonds (savings accounts and CDs are versions of bonds). Everything beyond stocks and bonds is a derivative.

Much of the investment world uses the first derivatives beyond stocks and bonds—mutual funds, closed-end funds, and exchange-traded funds. A few more sophisticated investors will use the next derivative—options, which I explained above. But beyond options is a whole list of forward contracts that the typical investor cannot even define and should avoid. A partial list includes mortgage-bond swaps (MBS), collateralized debt obligations (CDO), and credit default swaps (CDS). The total value of these financial instruments would go from under $38 trillion in 1999 to over $175 trillion in 2007. By comparison, the GDP (Gross Domestic Product) of the entire U.S. in 2007 was about $15 trillion. Thus, the Great Recession.

A few years before the 2007–2008 financial crisis, Warren Buffet was quoted as saying derivatives were "financial weapons of mass destruction." While some derivatives are listed on the commodity exchanges, none are listed on the major stock exchanges, and daily prices are scarce or not available at all. Derivatives such as these should always be avoided by the individual investor.

Mutual Funds and ETFs

Mutual funds were the only reasonable choice for beginning investors when I began my financial career. They still provide sound fundamental investments to investors who are starting out, but you have to make sure that the fund or combination of funds you invest in meets your preferred strategies—the diversification of stocks that you want, the particular sectors of the market that you have decided to invest in, and the level of risk you are willing to tolerate.

If you are invested in a managed account or fund, you should remember that all managers will underperform their chosen markets in some cycles. These periods of underperformance are not a good reason to fire the manager. Reviewing the manager's record or asking a professional to review it is good practice, but jumping from stock to stock, from fund to fund, or from manager to manager is acting in the short term when the objective is to think and act long term.

ETFs have become very popular in the last few years because they have low cost-ratios, come with some tax advantages, and most are designed to mirror a stated index—ETFs have made few capital gains distributions.

Beginning investors will find many advantages to owning funds rather than owning individual stocks. Buying funds allows investors to purchase more stocks at a lower price, creating more opportunities for diversification. Once you have achieved some success as an investor and have larger amounts to invest, then either funds or a portfolio of individual stocks can work for you.

Managed Accounts

Most good firms will have managed accounts as well as a selection of outside managers, and these accounts should provide the proper diversification, income, quality, and reporting that the investor needs.

An average investor not planning to become a financial specialist can easily rely on these accounts to provide a reasonable return in line with the level of risk selected—typically either growth, growth and income, or income. The differences between these account types come down to the level of risk you are willing to tolerate. While growth investments are good for increasing the value of an investment over time, the rate of growth is often unpredictable. Income investments, on the other hand, provide a steadier source of income on a regular basis, though the return may not be as high. Growth and income investments combine elements from each to provide a somewhat stable income with higher returns. A benefit of managed accounts is that there are generally less tax obligations than on mutual funds and ETFs.

Income

The whole point of investing is not to take part in a painful and stress-filled process but to secure your financial security by generating a new source of income. Once you have achieved your goals—once you can enjoy the benefits of accumulated assets representing the result of your hard work and savings—seeing your income stream in is especially rewarding.

Putting money in government-guaranteed CDs or short-term, high-grade bonds can be very boring, but a lot of investors begin with these types of investments. Collecting just 4 percent interest on $500,000 with a CD or similar investment will increase your income by $20,000 per year. That figure goes to $400,000 per year on $10,000,000. If you start with this basic premise, you are less likely to be enticed by claims of higher returns for riskier investments.

Once you select an advisor—which will be discussed in chapter 9—you will be investing in some combination of stocks and bonds or portfolios of them, such as managed accounts, mutual funds, or exchange-traded funds (ETFs). Your long-term investments will play out successfully if you abide by the things you have learned: You will diversify your investments. You will avoid trading and gambling. You will look to the long term and see market declines as buying opportunities instead of scary events. And you will enjoy the process.

Wise Investment Practices

Resisting Pressure from Family and Friends

In the book *The Millionaire Next Door: The Surprising Secrets of America's Wealthy*, the author explains how ordinary people have become wealthy by living below their income level and maintaining discipline with their assets.[1] You will need discipline in order to resist the pressure to lend or give money to friends or relatives, which can increase as you begin to accumulate assets. It is almost impossible to hide wealth from friends, and especially from family.

Selecting Professionals

More successful investment professionals will always provide more comfort. Almost all successful investors will eventually need a CPA, a financial advisor, and an attorney. If you have confidence in your investment advisor, the management of your assets, and the documentation, you can relax and start thinking longer-term.

Chapter 9 of this book addresses the considerations of selecting an advisor. While it is especially critical that an investor chooses well when selecting an advisor, the same can be said for choosing a CPA or attorney.

Tax Strategies

As you acquire more assets, tax planning becomes more complicated—and more important. There are a number of easily accessible tax-filing programs that can facilitate simple and direct filings for those with simple returns, such as TurboTax or H&R Block, but as you acquire more assets and pay more taxes, more complex tax strategies will need to be applied. Good professionals—CPAs and advisors—can provide proper instruction and assistance. The most important thing to remember is that proper documentation is a must.

Risk Assessment and Strategies

Whether you are a seasoned investor or a novice, and whether you manage your own investments or hire an advisor, managing your portfolio is ultimately your responsibility. An advisory service may have the fiduciary responsibility of managing your assets, but owning those assets still burdens you with making crucial decisions—including, for example, what level of risk you are comfortable with.

Chapter 8

The Role of Work

This book is not intended to give you a formula for good investing, but to help you avoid poor investment practices. However, there are some insights into making wise investments that you can learn along the way. One common denominator of good investors is that most put their money to work where good people will use it with skills, honesty, diligence, and intelligence.

I have given speeches and written articles on "the American workstation," or the conditions of employment in corporate America. I will not go into cost calculations for all the different corporate workstations, but let's just consider the rough cost of putting people to work. Workstation costs run from around $150,000 per work slot at Walmart to around $4 million at ExxonMobil. If you are a worker at any private or public entity, your boss or company has invested a lot of money to provide you with that job. Your employer has invested that money hoping to get a return on that capital. Your job is a service to that entity, and you can choose to be happy or unhappy in your attitude toward your work.

Some investor has laid out a great deal of money for your workstation. In current numbers, someone must own over 1,200 shares of Walmart to give just one person a job, and over 63,000 shares of

ExxonMobil to employ one worker. There is a lot more on the line in a job than just doing a day's assignment and collecting a paycheck.

The Opportunities of Wealth

The goal of most people is to reach a point in life where they do not have to work to live a fulfilling life. Those who are wealthy have already reached this point—they have the option of not working or, more importantly, working on the activity of their choice. It is the activity of choice that gives anyone a sense of fulfillment. Working in a charity, a foundation, a church, or any service organization can be a fulfilling activity, yet working in the production of something that contributes to the economy or society at large can be fulfilling as well.

The Risks of Inactivity

A life without activity exposes you to many negative mental and physical conditions. In a recent discussion about work, my son Spencer brought up a study that showed the use of alprazolam (Xanax) which is prescribed to lower the level of anxiety, is much higher among people with low levels of activity. We hear about people using drugs like Xanax or Valium or Tryptophan to address anxiety, but we hear almost nothing about getting up and doing something in order to lower your level of anxiety.

There are many accomplished people who credit the level of activity they have practiced for their success. In a great number of those cases, the level of activity includes regular trips to the gym, the running track, or the game court in addition to a high level of professional activity. Doing nothing, in contrast, can have mental, physical, and monetary consequences.

Choosing Happiness in Your Work

There are so many different kinds of work in the world. A single job description can encompass thousands of different jobs, and there is no type of work that precludes a higher level of activity. A retail clerk can become a department manager, who can become a store manager, who can become a corporate executive. A construction worker can become a carpenter, who can become a contractor. The list goes on and on, and there are millions of examples where an entry-level person has eventually moved up the ladder to a higher profession. Almost all of those cases will involve determination, persistence, and hard work by the successful employee, which can make achieving one's goals all the more sweet. In the long run, the achievement level—and career satisfaction—of the individual is far more dependent on individual work ethic than the choice of career.

As two often-quoted aphorisms say: "The only place where success comes before work is in the dictionary!" And, "Flipping burgers is not beneath your dignity. Your grandparents had a different word for burger flipping—they called it opportunity."

Productivity

In managing my staff, I always told them that two people could sit side by side doing the same job, and one could produce twice as much as the other—sometimes without a noticeable difference between their activity levels. In almost all those cases, the productive person is happier than the less productive person. This is where our individual choice comes into play.

A phrase that my grandson encouraged me to add to this book is "load the freight." It's a term I repurposed from one of my part-time jobs in the fields of East Texas, where I loaded pickup trucks heading for the market with tomato baskets. These vehicles could hold anywhere from sixteen to thirty baskets, depending on the size of the truck and whether side frames were in use.

Whether you are loading hay bales, processing paper, or returning phone calls, your individual work activity can range from more or less productive to downright lazy. I like to think of any kind of work as "loading the freight." It's easy to measure your work when you are loading trucks, but not so easy when you are evaluating reports, making phone calls, or creating documents. However, if you are honest with yourself, you know the pace of your work at any given time, and you will certainly be happier when you are more productive.

Whatever the conditions or circumstances of your employment, those conditions do not keep you from looking at the job with a positive attitude. We are all able to choose how we feel about our job and our life, and when we show happiness, the people around us tend to feel better about themselves and, hopefully, their jobs too.

Encouraging Quotes

According to Henry Ford, "Quality means doing it right when no one is looking." Choosing to do your job when no one is looking is key to your happiness and fulfillment at work. Henry Ford was an icon in mass production, but his understanding of the individual's sense of accomplishment was key to his success. He was known for how he inspired people to work with enthusiasm.

"Either you run the day or the day runs you," said Jim Rohn. It is easy to play the victim in your job or in many other aspects of your life. But if you accept where you are and assess your status properly, then you can begin to take control of what happens next and apply your skills to the tasks in front of you. You cannot change where you find yourself at any point in time, but you can certainly change how you react to the conditions around you. Your reaction can then change the outcome of the future.

Robert Frost said, "The best way out is always through." Frost was simply telling us to face up to where we are and consider that sometimes the best path may be the more difficult one. Many times, we spend more time and effort trying to skirt around a problem, when we would be better served by addressing it head on.

"Life is like riding a bicycle. To keep your balance, you must keep moving," according to Albert Einstein. This quote applies to life in general, but it is certainly applicable to your job. "Staying busy" is a cliché, but it is key to success and, yes, happiness.

It is easy to fall into inactivity. One of mine and my wife's favorite restaurants is always busy, and virtually all of the waiters and waitresses are constantly bussing tables, carrying food, and cleaning up. However, there is one waiter who is noticeably idle while those around him are rushing around. I wish I could help him see value in staying busy and enjoying his work. Many good restaurants will teach their servers to bus tables on their way to and from the kitchen, whether or not those tables are assigned to them. This level of customer service is key to the success of any business operation.

Work Ethic

Now to the task at hand. How do you approach work? It's sad how many young people in the current generation consider it an imposition to contribute to the workforce. What is our purpose if not to serve, to provide something helpful to our fellow citizens?

In the early days of this country, 90 percent of our people lived on the farm, versus about 10 percent today. Everyone in the family was expected to go out and produce something so that the family could eat. There are only a limited number of hours available per day, and our ancestors made use of every single one of them. A decision to plant forty rows of corn instead of twenty was a decision to work twice as hard in the corn patch that particular season.

In your office today, you have a similar choice. You can choose to make five client calls, or you can expand that to ten. You know that every client call will likely lead to some amount of follow-up work, and that will increase your workload. You can decide to produce five pages of material today, or you might decide to shoot for ten. How much you accomplish is very often a decision on your part, rather than something dictated by your boss or circumstances. You can grudgingly do a minimum amount of work, or you can choose to do more than is assigned and expected of you. How much money you make is only a temporary measurement that varies depending on many factors, like seniority, profitability, or management. You should not let any of those factors be an excuse for a lack of productivity.

Remember when I worked in that hardware store in high school and rebuilt the shelves? I found this a much more productive use of my time than waiting around for customers, and I spent several months rebuilding all the wall shelving, all the counters, and the central office. The owner and the managers were excited, and I felt more useful. I do not recall whether my income increased as a result of my extra work, but I do know that my skills improved, my job became more important and fulfilling, and I saved money to pay for college.

A Point System

Over all my years in business and even now in retirement, I keep a tally of my daily activities and give myself points for projects completed, papers processed, calls made, and other productive activities. I give myself a point goal for each day as well as a minimum total, which I label "criminally negligent." Employees on my staff were encouraged to approach their work in the same way—find a way to measure how well you are working. One often-heard phrase is "Fail to plan, plan to fail." That simple phrase demonstrates the importance of approaching every task with a plan, for without one, the best of intentions descend into chaos.

If you are idle to the point of having nothing to do, then you need to evaluate your attitude toward your job. A retail clerk who isn't seeing a lot of customers, for example, can work on the presentation of merchandise, cleaning the facility, or even getting more traffic through the door. On any day that he doesn't have a paying job, a carpenter can work on his own place, sharpen tools at his workbench, and call prospective customers. If you're unemployed, you can work on job applications, exercise, or do maintenance on your residence, whether it is rented or owned. And anyone can find a way to help others in their spare time by volunteering individually or through an organization.

Spending a lot of idle time in any job is evidence of a very poor imagination. No matter your task or position, it is imperative that you determine how you can be of service and then allocate your time wisely. If using your time wisely means finding a way to measure your work, then that is what you should do—maybe even develop a point system for yourself.

All work is service—we achieve happiness by serving others. When you provide excellent service, you contribute to your own happiness and gain personal fulfillment.

Chapter 9

Selecting an Advisor

For anyone starting out in investing, it is of the utmost importance that you select a financial advisor. Yet there are many considerations that must go into this decision. Your choice may be limited by the amount of funds you have to invest—any investor with less than $100,000 will receive less attention than one with $300,000, and an investor with $300,000 will receive less attention than one with $500,000 or more. Many of the large investment firms will further restrict their advisors to accounts with a minimum of $300,000, $500,000, $1,000,000, or even more. Those with less are considered "small investors," but that does not mean that they are not important.

It's critical that small investors adhere to the basic principles laid out in this book, primarily maintaining liquid assets and diversifying investments. Most small investors should be in major mutual funds or ETFs, and if a small investor is in a managed account, the portfolio should have at least twenty-five stocks, contain several industry sectors, and include primarily large companies that pay dividends. The small investor must ask good questions before committing any hard-earned assets, such as where your assets will be held and what type of access you will have to your funds. There are good resources available to help small investors make good choices, but it is no simple matter to find and evaluate the relevant information. This is where a financial advisor can be very helpful.

Let's look at an example. I hold stocks in corporation X—I remember a high around $30 and a low around $20, but I have no clue as to the earnings either this or the previous year. I certainly have no clue what earnings to expect the following year. If I see a P/E ratio of 14 on my stock currently, is that below its industry average, is it above, or is it about the same? And how about growth? The math is simple, but the numbers can be very elusive. If my advisor has good resources, he or she can tell me what to expect. Will the numbers show growth? Will the numbers show a decline? And where is the industry going? An advisor with good resources can tell you a lot about your stock's current performance, as well as expectation for the ensuing years.

There is no magic in these reports. There will be errors because the analysts are humans, and there is no way of knowing everything, but these are professional people with good resources, experiences, and educations who are looking at companies with a lot more information than you or I have. They have files and records on the companies and industries, not to mention information on the company managers. We cannot rely on everything we see in an analyst report, but those reports do help with our investment strategies.

It is important to diversify your investments because there is no assurance that you will have 100 percent accurate information, and there is no guarantee that a currently flourishing industry will continue to experience success in the future. However, the more access my advisor has to financial resources, the more I can rely on their guidance.

Asset Custody

Almost all investment advisory and brokerage firms offer a service that houses account investments at the Depository Trust Company (DTC). The Depository Trust Company and the National Securities Clearing

Corporation (NSCC) are both owned and managed by the Depository Trust & Clearing Corporation (DTCC), which is overseen by the SEC. The U.S. government provides security for these entities.

Most companies will not issue paper certificates today, and stock ownership is instead primarily in digital form and must be housed in some database. In the United States, this takes the form of the DTC, while Europe has the European Central Security Depositories Association (ECSDA).

In all Ponzi schemes and most investment advisor scandals, the victims are tricked into putting their money in some entity that exists outside the DTC. Once you place your money in an entity that is not housed in a bank or DTC-custody facility, the liquidity of your investment drops and the risk goes up. There are many great investments in the private sector, but the average investor does not have the resources to evaluate them.

If a U.S. investor buys a stock or bond through a registered dealer, the security is automatically housed at the DTC. But when an investor goes outside a registered dealer, the asset custody is in question. Who controls the gold bars that I buy? Who houses the uninsured CDs? Where will I store the diamonds? What happens if the investment firm fails? What happens if my bank fails?

In every economic cycle, there are failures of investment firms and banks. When an investment firm fails, the fact that my securities are housed at the DTC provides me with a great amount of protection, because the accounts can be picked up by any of the many other securities firms in the country. It's still important, however, to work with a firm that has a good financial history. The largest custodian in the United States is currently the Bank of New York Mellon, and many investment advisory firms use this bank or a similar major custodian. These custodians give the clients of smaller firms continued asset security, and they provide clearing activity for investment accounts.

When a bank fails, the Federal Reserve is responsible for all FDIC-insured accounts. There may be a waiting period while all the assets are being sorted out, but it is usually just a matter of weeks before the proceeds of the account are paid out to the owner. However, any funds above the insured limits are subject to allocation or are lost entirely, and so individual depositors should be aware of any funds that exceed the insured limits. Yet corporate deposits are subject to the same insurance limits, so CFOs must be extremely careful when keeping up with the balance sheet of a bank their company is invested in. A $250,000 deposit insurance is of little value to a company that might have millions of dollars in deposits at any one bank.

Liquidity

Knowing the liquidity of an investment is critical to knowing how to access your money. Cash is liquid. The liquidity of a savings account depends on the fine print. A CD is considered a semi-liquid investment, but the cash-out conditions can cost a lot of money. A good bond is usually considered a liquid investment, but a big uptick in the interest rate can change its value overnight. However, a high-quality bond is almost always available for sale at the market price.

But there are other investments whose liquidity is much more questionable. We saw in chapter 6 how risky the CDs of non-insured banks can be. In an economic downturn, the liquidity of those investments can be almost nonexistent.

Depending on what assets you own, here are some questions you may need to ask:

- How do I sell my gold or diamonds when I need cash?
- How do I cash out my investment?
- How do I lease or sell my real estate?

Enhancing Your Resources

We often make important investment decisions without consulting anyone. But why do we consider that our knowledge is superior to that of the rest of the world? Do I always know what fertilizer is best for my grass? Do I know what current drugs are best for high blood pressure? Do I know whether my air conditioner only needs Freon, or if it needs replacing entirely? Having just a semi-intelligent source of advice, someone with resources and experience to inform your decisions, will improve your results.

A Professional Salesman

Is your financial advisor a salesman? Hopefully, yes. All professional salesmen are educators who match good information with the user's needs. Is my doctor a salesman? If he has a good bedside manner, the answer is yes.

If I asked you to produce a ten-year chart on Microsoft, could you do that? Maybe. But if I asked you to compare that same chart on Microsoft with those of other software companies, could you do that? Probably not.

It is entirely proper to take advice from someone who can be gently convincing when suggesting an intelligent investment move.

How to Choose an Advisor

Selecting an advisor is a critical part of being a responsible investor and keeping your money. Many investment advisors—and doctors, and lawyers, and contractors—are serving prison time because they have betrayed their profession. The numbers will vary, but fortunately the abusers are a very small fraction of the professionals in this country. Still, you should not hesitate to ask for the biography and history of the person you are evaluating to provide long-term advice.

In 2020, Northwestern Mutual did a study and found that 71 percent of U.S. adults believe their financial planning could be improved, but only 29 percent of Americans have a financial advisor.[1]

A later Vanguard study found that on average, a $500K investment could grow to $3.4 million over twenty-five years under the care of an experienced financial advisor, whereas the expected value from self-management would be only $1.69 million.[2] An advisor-managed portfolio averages 8 percent annualized growth over that period, compared to 5 percent from a self-managed one.

Here are some important questions to consider when choosing an advisor:

- *Will the majority of my assets be housed at the DTC or in an FDIC-insured account?* Throughout this book I have stressed the importance of owning liquid securities that are housed at the DTC in your name. Any assets that are in an account not belonging to you are at a higher risk, because you have little recourse upon losing your money.

- *Does this advisor have a criminal record?* In today's world, anyone can make a claim against anyone on almost anything, and many of those claims will be on public records. Actual criminal convictions, however, are another story, and multiple convictions or even multiple accusations are red flags. You can easily go online and search for a financial advisor's record.

- *Will this person assure that my account is diversified?* As I've stressed multiple times, diversification is key to any successful investing strategy. Any advisor who professes to know the best single investment should be evaluated with caution.

- *Is this person stable?* It is not unusual for advisors to switch firms, especially to upgrade the services he or she can offer. If, however, an advisor has a history of moving often from firm to firm, that can be a red flag. The typical contract that a professional might sign when moving to a new firm requires the person to stay for at least a three-year period. If the advisor has moved from firm to firm every three years, that should raise a caution flag, as instability in one's job can also show up in one's work.

- *Is this person speaking first of liquid investments?* Any investment professional who begins a conversation with a prospect by bringing up great opportunities in "special products" and "private ventures" should be regarded cautiously. A truly professional advisor will spend time talking about the allocation and diversification of assets across liquid investments and the long-term nature of responsible investing.

- *What will I pay?* It is critical that you ask for the costs associated with your account before depositing any money with your advisor. Fee-based accounts are the most common in today's investment world, and the rate is usually based on the size of your account. Investors with over a million dollars are fortunate because their accounts charge well under 1 percent in fees. The costs go up for smaller accounts, but in no case should the total cost of an account exceed 2 percent per year. Some firms, however, will charge an annual fee, with a percentage of assets among other costs added on top.

- *What resources are available to my advisor?* The main benefit of working with an investment advisor is not only their wealth of experience but their access to critical resources. Any good advisor will have access to a good custodian for assets as well as research on securities including stocks, bonds, mutual funds, and ETFs.

Mistakes to Avoid

In 2023, the online publication *SmartAsset* listed seven mistakes people make in selecting a financial advisor.[3] Here they are:

1. *Hiring an advisor who is not a fiduciary.* A fiduciary financial advisor is "ethically bound to act in another person's best interest." In most cases, a fiduciary will handle assets on a fee-based schedule that is easily available to the investor.

2. *Hiring the first advisor you meet.* Lack of dedication and attention in the process of hiring a financial advisor can be costly. Advisors are just like any other professional, and they often

have a specialty—some advisors will only take accounts over $10 million, while others may only handle retirement accounts. It's critical that you do the research to select the advisor that is best for you and your assets.

3. *Choosing an advisor with the wrong specialty.* Many advisors specialize in serving a particular customer base. For example, some advisors specialize in corporate pension plans, while others are better at managing individual investments. You need to make sure your candidate specializes in investors like you, with your size and type of assets.

4. *Picking an advisor with an incompatible strategy.* Similar to the last mistake, some advisors will concentrate on specific segments of the market or even on particular classes of investments besides stocks and bonds. Some advisors, for example, specialize in commodities, while others work more with CDs or annuities.

5. *Not asking about credentials.* The minimum credentials for a financial advisor are passing the Series 6 Exam, which licenses the sale of mutual funds and annuities, among other investment products, as well as the Series 7, or General Securities Exam. You should never hire anyone who is not a registered financial advisor. Additional certificates might be the Certified Financial Planner (CFP), the Certified Investment Management Analyst (CIMA), or an insurance license. All of these are great additions to an advisor's credentials, and many advisory teams will include advisors with one or more of these additional certificates.

6. *Not understanding how they are paid.* While most financial advisory accounts are fee-based, it is common in larger accounts to separate out some additional holdings for the advisor's compensation. These might include large corporate positions acquired in the course of an investor's career or large bond holdings that the investor does not plan to sell. Investors should beware, however, as accounts that stray from this standard system are

more prone to distortions in performance, as large positions can violate our quest for diversification.

7. *Not hiring a vetted advisor.* If you want to be a serious investor, you need to take the time to check out an advisor's credentials and become personally familiar with the advisor before allowing them to handle your life accumulations.

Paying for the Advice

Most account management fees range from around 1.5 percent if you're a small investor to as low as 0.35 percent if you have many millions in an account. A few years ago I was at a meeting with BlackRock, the largest asset manager in the world, and they began the meeting by telling us the world was migrating to a 35-basis-point fee level. They were of course speaking about fees on high net-worth accounts—those that are over the $10-million-dollar threshold.

When I was first introduced to mutual funds, the majority of funds had a front-end load, or a one-time sales charge that is paid upfront. That load began at 8.5 percent and declined to as little as 1 percent for multi-million-dollar transactions. Then there were also annual management fees that could range up or down from 1 percent, depending upon the size of the holding. If you were paying over 8 percent to begin an investment, there was no question that the investment should be viewed as long, long term. Fortunately, the front-end load and management fees have declined as technology progressed.

Today, the small investor should be prepared to pay a total of 1 percent or higher in management fees. In many cases, that total is the sum of an upfront fee plus the annual management fees for the funds held in the account. For example, an upfront fee of 1 percent plus a mutual fund fee of 0.5 percent will cost the investor a total of 1.5 percent in the first year. Many ETFs will have management fees as low as 0.15 percent, although a recent study showed the average to be around 0.4 percent. Some online services even advertise a zero-fee schedule, yet we should keep in mind that all businesses need revenue and there are other sources to fund all these zero-cost accounts, which the investors will pay—whether hidden or openly displayed.

All investors should ask how much they are paying. If you pay a 1 percent total annual fee on an account, that fee will provide for the research as well as the custody and movement of your assets. At a 1 percent rate, those costs are easily offset by good-quality advice.

Advice to the Advisor

None of us would take our car to the dealership without providing important information about its performance and maintenance. We would not go to our doctor without sharing everything we know about our ailments. The same goes for the advisor we choose—there are some key details that your advisor must know to properly manage our investments.

Assets

There is often a temptation to only tell your advisor about some of your assets—just the assets you want to invest, or the assets your advisor helps manage. But the more you hold back, the less the advisor will be able to help you. It is imperative, for example, that the advisor or advisory team know whether you have a savings account before you start investing, as well as whether or not you have other investment accounts. The CPA and the estate attorney should also be advised of all your assets.

Changes in Your Spending

Whether you have been with an advisor for two weeks or two years, it is important that you tell your advisor about any changes in your spending. That is especially true if there might be a need to liquidate cash from your investments.

Tax Status

Income changes will change your tax status, and so you should keep your CPA and financial advisor updated on any changes to your income. These would include losing a job, receiving a promotion, marrying or getting a divorce, or inheriting a sum of money. You should alert your accountant, your financial advisor, and possibly your estate attorney to any of these changes.

Allocation

Your attitude and tolerance for market swings is a huge factor in how your advisor guides your investments. You should discuss your level of risk tolerance with your advisor so that your account can be properly slanted toward growth, growth and income, or mostly income. And you should know that new investors may not realize how frightening it can be when the markets are down 30, 40, or 50 percent. If you change your mind about how much risk you are willing to tolerate, be sure to update your advisor!

Documentation

Key documents that should be part of a responsible investor's communication with an advisor include 1) your beneficiary selections, 2) your will, 3) a revocable family living trust (a trust that can be changed or dissolved at any time—this document will be appropriate if the family has a spendthrift member), 4) the name and number of your CPA, 5) the name and number of your attorney, and 6) your gifting plans.

Giving your advisor your key financial documents and keeping them apprised of all changes in your personal finances is key to good communication.

Chapter 10

Finding Happiness

Throughout this book I have given examples of what can go wrong with your wealth. I have not offered a magic formula for investing, but I have explained a few positive things that successful investors do correctly. And on the principle that if you really want to drive a point home you have to say it, say you said it, and then say it one more time, in this final chapter I want to sum up the wise things you should be doing if you want to *keep your money*.

It's Not Rocket Science

Keeping your money is much more about personal discipline than science or strategy. The behaviors you should practice are very simple, but small violations can have serious long-term consequences. You are encouraged to use this chapter to evaluate how you are doing in maintaining good discipline.

Maintain Liquidity

The portfolios of good stocks and investment-grade bonds are very liquid and will provide cash flow, as are funds made up of these securities.

Most importantly, all of these securities are housed at the DTC and will continue to be listed in your name even if the investment firm fails.

As an investor myself, I never put more than 1 percent of my assets in any private, non-liquid investment, and I've never had more than 5 percent of my total assets in these ventures. My advice to clients was to never exceed 10 percent in non-liquid assets.

Diversify

None of the brilliant, highly educated economists and analysts know when the stock market will go down or which sectors of the economy will tank, and this is precisely why you must diversify your investments across not only multiple companies but multiple industries as well. At the time of this writing, the S&P 500 index lists eleven different sectors, and almost every category listing shows between eight and twenty different subcategories. A good portfolio will include many of these categories. While small investors may struggle to own individual stocks in enough of these categories, mutual funds and ETFs can provide effective diversification. Larger investors can own portfolios of individual stocks and bonds with higher levels of diversification.

We can argue about the numbers later, but let's look at some suggested minimums. In order to be reasonably diversified in stocks, you should own a minimum of about twenty stocks across at least five different sectors. All your CDs should be under the FDIC-insured limit—today it is $250,000—and bonds should be investment-grade or above. Rating agencies S&P and Fitch use ratings from AAA all the way down to D, for "default." Moody's, the other major rating agency, goes from Aaa down to Baa3 and all the way to C for their default level. Investment-grade bonds are considered a safe investment, but diversification is also important here, and staying above the minimum investment-grade level is very important. And remember from chapter 5 that longer-term maturities can carry much larger risks. Smaller investors should consider investment-grade bond funds in order to achieve diversification.

Spend Less Than You Make

It seems obvious that, without inherited assets, you must save money in order to accumulate wealth. There are many cases where people with moderate or even small incomes have become millionaires. The key behavior in this endeavor is to live within your means—and that means spending less than you bring in.

Spending less than you make sounds simple enough. But with every major purchase you increase your cost of living, because every item comes with a maintenance cost. A big house has big taxes, big insurance costs, and big repair costs. An expensive car requires more insurance and expensive repairs. Even a sturdy piece of furniture must be refurbished at some point in time. Recognizing that every purchase carries a maintenance cost is key to spending wisely.

Live without Credit Card Debt

Avoiding credit card debt is crucial to financial success. The availability of credit on these cards can be very tempting, but the interest on credit card debt is typically three to four times what a bank will charge. When there is something that you really want or believe your family really needs, it is easy to whip out the credit card and purchase that item. However, it's not so easy to make the payments on that purchase. At a typical 20-percent interest rate, the annual interest cost on a $10,000 credit-card debt amounts to $2,000. That's $2,000 not going into savings, not getting used for necessities, and, depending on how long that debt lasts, decreasing your standard of living for a long time.

I grew up in the age before credit cards became a part of all family possessions. And at that time it was not commonly accepted to borrow money from the bank for normal spending—bank loans were reserved for cars and necessary appliances. Sellers would often extend credit for purchases, but a live person was on duty to discuss your needs and ability to pay back the debt.

Let's put this problem in real terms. A person making $50,000 per year has a reasonable income. But if that person runs up a $30,000 credit card debt, the typical interest is $6,600 per year, and the typical required payment is $1,525 per month (this amount is set by each credit card company, but it is typically determined by using the interest rate plus a payoff in ten years)—that equals $18,300 per year. The borrower has committed over one-third of their entire income to paying off this credit card debt. Over one-third of their standard of living is gone for the next several months or even years. Credit card debt can ruin a person's finances for a long time.

Always Have Cash on Hand

This rule sounds simple, but it can make the difference between being prepared and having every emergency become an ongoing problem. Of course, by having cash on hand I don't mean carrying around physical dollar bills and coins in your pocket, but maintaining access to liquid funds that you can easily use when it becomes necessary. If you spend less than your income, you will have some cash in savings. If you never carry credit card debt, you are likely to have cash available. There are unforeseen expenses in everyone's life, like emergencies or surprise repair bills. Friends and relatives may depend upon you when they have an emergency. When you have cash available, surprise expenses become events instead of emergencies.

I was once in Connecticut attending a training course for financial-firm branch managers. At dinner one evening, after a session on cash management, one of the managers said that he had never been without cash. He said, "My family never had much money, but I have always been able to have a cash reserve. Whenever I considered myself short of cash, I found a way to work more and earn more money." This person had gone on to be a very successful corporate manager. His message was very simple: watch your money and make sure to always have cash on hand.

We see so many advertisements telling us to "buy now and pay later," but those ads almost always hide some excessive mark-up or high interest expenses. If we pay as we go, we don't have to worry about hidden costs—and we are not buying now only to be frugal later.

In chapter 2, I laid out the hazards of spending your principal. When you avoid spending principal, you can begin saving—and always have cash.

Avoid Scams

In chapter 3, you read about all kinds of scams. If you are alert to the symptoms, it is less likely that you will ever fall victim to a scam. Scammers will appeal to some anxiety—whether it be romantic feelings or loneliness, monetary loss, or even monetary gain. They will ask for personal data and find a way to take your money.

Do the Paperwork

There are many good professionals in any industry, from contractors to medical professionals, who do not progress because they fail to write up proper quotes, do proper billing, and make their work known—and personal finance advisors are no exception.

As any legitimate financial advisor will tell you, taxes should be filed properly and on time. Wills, living, wills, and powers of attorney may sound boring, but they are extremely important documents. Family members and financial advisors should have copies of these documents, or files showing their location. And all these documents should be updated whenever there are changes in your family status or financial situation changes.

Avoid Gambling

This is not the first time in this book that I have told you to avoid gambling. Beyond your pocket money or dedicated entertainment budget, any cash spent at the card tables is gambling that will jeopardize a good investment plan. But gambling is not limited to casinos. Short-term trading is also considered gambling, and it should be avoided as such.

Always remember that the only reason to own an investment is its ultimate ability to pay you an income—whether it be rent, dividends, or interest. Buying a stock just to sell it quickly at a higher profit is gambling. As the saying goes, "There are bold traders, and there are old traders, but there are no old, bold traders." Being alert for bargains is an admirable investment practice. However, buying without the intent to own is a very poor practice. Another old saying is that you "should not marry a stock." An investment should be looked upon as a piece of equipment that is capable of producing income, not as a piece in a prize collection. Much like a vehicle, if that piece of equipment ceases to function properly, it should be changed. Yet it's even more important to remember that investments should be considered only for the long term—not for short-term gambling. In chapter 3, you saw the huge amounts of money that wealthy people have lost in gambling. Do not let this temptation ruin the lives of you and those around you!

Hold Good Investments during a Bear Market

If I could hang a plaque on your wall, it would say, Do Not Sell Good Stocks During a Bear Market. In my many decades in the investment advisory business, I have seen more money lost in violation of this principle than any other way.

It is during tough times that we get the most unsolicited advice, especially from those who have not built large assets of their own. This advice can come from family, friends, or outside opportunists, yet most of them don't actually know what they're talking about. For this reason, it's vital that you have a trusted financial advisor who can guide you through good times and bad.

A report by Fidelity Investments advises, "Stay invested: Don't risk missing the market's best days."[1] Their study covered the period from

January 1, 1980, to December 31, 2022, and tracked the performance of a $10,000 investment. That investment, invested in the market 100 percent of the time, would be worth $1.09 million at the end of that time period. Yet missing just the best five days of the market brought the net return down to $671,051—that reduced the entire return by 38 percent. Missing the best ten days took the amount down to $483,336, reduced by 56 percent. Being out of the market on the best thirty days reduced the amount to $173,695, and the best fifty days to $76,104. Let's look at them in a table:

Amount Invested	Period Invested	Net Return	Percent Difference
$10,000	January 1, 1980 – December 31, 2022 (in continuity)	$1,090,000	
$10,000	January 1, 1980 – December 31, 2022 (missing the best 5 days)	$671,051	38%
$10,000	January 1, 1980 – December 31, 2022 (missing the best 10 days)	$483,336	56%
$10,000	January 1, 1980 – December 31, 2022 (missing the best 30 days)	$173,695	84%
$10,000	January 1, 1980 – December 31, 2022 (missing the best 50 days)	$76,104	93%

While you consider the number above, think about this as well: multiple studies have shown that 34 percent of the best days in the stock market occur during the first two months after a bear-market bottom.

The most common excuses we hear for selling good stocks during bad times are that "I couldn't risk taking more loss" or "I needed the money." But the relevant principle is that you should buy only what you are prepared to own through a bear market.

Live on Your Income

When making an effort to live within your means, the first step is to calculate what exactly your means are, and then prepare a budget that fits those means. Newlyweds and new families are often faced with buying houses, cars, and other necessities. However, those decisions are often made in the expectation that incomes will increase substantially and without interruption. In most of these cases, the income expectations cause buyers to overshoot reality, resulting in several years of adjustment. Many of us spent our college years in a ten-by-twelve-foot room studying and trying to convince our significant others that better days were ahead. Our soldiers also know what it is like to live in small quarters with little spending. However, the tendency to overspend affects virtually everyone, and it is not until you have adjusted your spending level to match your income that the real savings can begin. Living on less than your income allows you to save and invest with pride.

Invest Wisely

In chapter 2, I explained asset accumulation and the value of dollar-cost averaging. This system of constant savings will give you a nice return on your investments through the ups and downs of share prices. For example, a decline of one-third in a share price will give a 50 percent return upon a recovery to the original price, while a decline of half the value will give a 100 percent return—doubling in value. In the early years, practicing accumulation can be even more valuable than choosing the right investments. Good mutual funds or ETFs can provide the diversification that you need during this phase of savings and accumulation.

Patience Is Golden

It is a fact that most fortunes are built over a long, long period of time. Keep in mind that the four-hundred-year average return on investments, going back to Europe before there was a United States, has been approximately 10 percent on equity (stocks) and 5 percent on borrowed money (savings accounts, CDs, and bonds). Every period is different, but it is amazing how these numbers tend to revert to the average. Ideally, you will start to save and invest early in life. However, later is far better than never, especially given that the typical investor makes most of their money later in life. Wherever you are in your investment journey, I hope and trust that the advice in this book will help you *keep your money*.

Acknowledgments

Thanks to all those who have helped me in developing this book.

First to my son, Spencer McGowan, who runs the investment-advisory firm McGowan Group. I have occasionally appeared on his radio show, *NetWorth Radio*, which airs on Saturdays and Sundays in Dallas, and I am sure that some of the financial information and ideas from the show may appear in this book, for which I thank him. I am also grateful for his generous assistance in writing *Keeping Your Money*, particularly for his contributions in drafting my personal story in the introduction.

Next, I want to thank four MBA students at the University of Texas at Dallas whom I was fortunate enough to mentor and who researched various topics that appear in this book: Marcine Pappiez, Batim Begzati, Doratina Begzati, and Frane Vidosevic. These students made multiple contributions to this book, including the charts on savings in chapter 2. Tina Begzati also contributed much of the story on the Fyre Festival in chapter 3.

Finally, I would like to thank my publisher, Brown Books Publishing Group, who took every care to see that this book was the best it could be.

Glossary

These terms are defined specifically for investment purposes; there is no attempt here to cover other definitions or uses.

401(k) — The pension plan at a U.S. corporation. Money is deducted from payroll and deposited into a 401(k) before the income is taxed. All earnings in the plan will grow without taxation and become taxable only when withdrawn from the plan and paid to the owner. Retiring individuals can "roll over" funds from a 401(k) to an IRA (Individual Retirement Account) without being taxed. The same plans for teachers are labeled 403(b), and those for government workers are 457(b) plans.

advisor — A registered financial professional who advises investors.

annuity — An insurance contract guaranteeing an income to the buyer.

art — A painting, sculpture, or other work deemed to carry an investment value.

bear market — A stock market decline that exceeds 20 percent. Every index is different, so it is possible that the QQQ, for example, can be in a bear market while other indices may not be.

black swan — A generally unknown risk that can cause severe declines in the stock market or the economy. The black swan in the 2007–2008 decline was the unknown size of the derivative market.

borrowing — Using someone else's money and paying interest.

compound interest — The increase in the value of an investment. All of our investments are measured by an annual rate. Using "the Rule of 72," a 1 percent rate of compound interest would double our investment in about 72 years. A 10 percent rate would double our investment in about 7.2 years. This rule is an approximate measurement, but it gives a good idea of how compounding works.

concentration — The investment of a great portion of one's assets in one investment or in a single sector of the market.

credit card — A card used to purchase any item or service on money borrowed from a bank. The billing will include interest if the balance is not paid every month.

Depository Trust Company (DTC) — An agency run by the U.S. government that is a member of the Federal Reserve and a clearing agency for all trades monitored by the Securities & Exchange Commission (SEC). The DTC holds all securities that are registered on any of the U.S. national exchanges.

derivatives — Forward contracts on the values of financial instruments.

diversification — Spreading assets among various stocks and asset categories.

dollar-cost averaging — The practice of investing the same amount of money at equal segments of time over a long period.

Dow Jones — The original stock index in the United States, consisting of thirty of the most prominent companies in corporate America. The index is weighted by price, which means that the higher-priced stocks carry a higher weight. For example, a $200 stock will carry four times the weight in the index of a $50 stock.

exchange traded funds (ETFs) — Mutual funds traded on a major exchange and consisting of replicas of an index, or defined portfolio. The funds are rebalanced at the end of each trading day and carry a relatively low cost ratio.

FAANG — An index of stocks that include Facebook (now Meta), Amazon, Apple, Netflix, and Google.

Federal Deposit Insurance Corporation (FDIC) — The government agency that, under the direction of the Federal Reserve, provides insurance for small investors. The agency was set up after the banking collapse of 1929 to protect the deposits of individuals, up to a limit. At the time of this writing, accounts at each bank are insured up to $250,000 by the FDIC. Joint accounts carry insurance up to $500,000. Trust accounts can be insured for up to five participants—$250,000 each, up to $1,250,000.

Federal Reserve — The Central Bank of the United States, often called the Fed.

growth — The category of stocks that exceed the annual growth of the economy.

illiquid investments — Investments that are not traded on an active exchange and do not have an instant cash value. Quotes have wide markups between the bid and asked prices.

index — An average of the price of all components in a specific list of investments. The major stock indexes are the Dow Jones, the S&P 500, the NASDAQ 100, and the Wilshire 5000. The Dow Jones is price weighted, while the S&P, NASDAQ, and Wilshire 5000 are all capital weighted, so that the value of the company determines its value in the index (see *weighted average* below). The Wilshire is a listing of all the actively traded stocks and currently includes about 3,800 stocks instead of 5,000.

individual retirement account (IRA) — An account that contains pre-tax funds deposited on a formula basis from the earned income of self-employed workers. Similar to a 401(k), earning accumulate tax-free since deposits are made prior to taxes, and funds can be rolled over by retiring workers without paying taxes. Withdrawals are taxed and must start after the age of seventy-two or seventy-three years of age, based upon average life expectancies.

Magnificent Seven — A group of seven stocks that dominated the S&P index and dominated its performance for much of 2023 and 2024, including Apple, Amazon, Google, Tesla, Nvidia, and Meta.

managed accounts — Investment accounts that are managed by an investment firm, an advisor, or some other party that is not the owner of the assets.

margin — Investing with borrowed money.

mutual fund — A portfolio of securities packaged and sold to individual investors.

Nifty Fifty — A group of fifty stocks in the 1970s that were considered the most trustworthy and dependable of the entire array of available stocks in the U.S.

penny stocks — Stocks that trade under $1 in price.

QQQ — An ETF that mirrors the NASDAQ 100 stock index. The index is heavily weighted towards Big Tech stocks, with Tech accounting for 60 percent of the value and the highest-weighted stock being seventy-eight times the value of the smallest.

Roth IRA — An Individual Retirement Account funded with post-tax dollars and not taxed upon distribution. Legislation allows a person to convert IRA and 401(k) funds to a Roth IRA by paying income taxes when the funds are converted.

S&P 500 — The index made up of five hundred of the most prominent companies in the U.S. economy. The Standard & Poor's company decides which five hundred stocks belong in the index.

trading — The act of buying or shorting something with the intent of making a short-term profit.

value — The category of high-equity, high-income, and dividend-paying stocks.

weighted average — An average price of securities in an index or portfolio in which more weight is given to stocks according to their price or their total worth—in contrast to an equal average, which gives the same weight to all the stocks in the index or portfolio.

will — A properly executed document that defines what heirs get from the estate of a deceased person. A living will, on the other hand, is a document that determines how medical attention is provided to someone who is considered incompetent or near death.

Notes

Chapter 1

1. Fidelity Investments, "Stay invested: Don't risk missing the market's best days," https://www.fidelity.com/bin-public/060_www_fidelity_com/documents/dont-miss-best-days.pdf.

Chapter 3

1. Mark Huffman, "Here are the top 10 scams of 2022," *ConsumerAffairs*, October 24, 2022, https://www.consumeraffairs.com/news/here-are-the-top-10-scams-of-2022-102422.html.
2. Nick Fountain and Mitch Zuckoff, "Charles Ponzi's scheme," *Planet Money* (podcast), NPR, January 20, 2023, https://aut.ac.nz.libguides.com/c.php?g=685064&p=5255905.
3. Chase Peterson-Withorn, *Forbes*, "The Investors Who Had To Pay Back Billions In Ill-Gotten Gains From Bernie Madoff's Ponzi Scheme," April 14, 2021, https://www.forbes.com/sites/chase-withorn/2021/04/14/the-investors-who-had-to-pay-back-billions-in-ill-gotten-gains-from-bernie-madoffs-ponzi-scheme/.

4. Diana B. Henriques, "Lapses Helped Schemes, Madoff Told Investigators," *New York Times,* October 30, 2009, https://www.nytimes.com/2009/10/31/business/31sec.html.

5. John Stepek, "How the tulip mania of 1636 became the mother of all bubbles," *MoneyWeek*, November 3, 2017, https://moneyweek.com/475864/how-the-tulip-mania-of-1636-became-the-mother-of-all-bubbles.

6. Charles Mackay, *Extraordinary Popular Delusions & the Madness of Crowds* (New York: Crown Trade Paperbacks, 1995).

7. Brad Smithfield, "Victor Lustig – the con man who sold the Eiffel Tower twice…," The Vintage News, 2016, https://www.thevintage-news.com/2016/10/23/victor-lustig-the-con-man-who-sold-the-eiffel-tower-twice/.

8. Tom Huddleston Jr., "Fyre Festival: How a 25-year-old scammed investors out of $26 million," *CNBC*, August 18, 2019, https://www.cnbc.com/2019/08/18/how-fyre-festivals-organizer-scammed-in-vestors-out-of-26-million.html.

9. Nick Igbokwe, "What happened to Vince Young? Former Titans QB's love for Cheesecake Factory wipes out over $25 million," *Sportskeeda*, modified April 13, 2023, https://www.sportskeeda.com/nfl/news-what-happened-vince-young-former-titans-qb-s-love-cheesecake-factory-wipes-25-million.

10. Pablo S. Torre, "How (and Why) Athletes Go Broke," *Sports Illustrated*, "Vault" archives, March 23, 2009, https://vault.si.com/vault/2009/03/23/how-and-why-athletes-go-broke.

11. Billboard Staff, "Michael Jackson Died Deeply in Debt," *Billboard*, June 26, 2009, https://www.billboard.com/music/music-news/michael-jackson-died-deeply-in-debt-268276/.

12. Nancy Dillon, "Michael Jackson was on verge of bankruptcy before death, banker testifies in court," *Daily News,* updated April 8, 2018, https://www.nydailynews.com/2017/02/07/michael-jackson-was-on-verge-of-bankruptcy-before-death-banker-testifies-in-court/.

13. Joe McGauley, "Everything MC Hammer Blew His Fortune On,"

Thrillist, March 30, 2014, https://www.thrillist.com/home/why-mc-hammer-went-broke-how-mc-hammer-spent-all-of-his-money.

14. Aya Tsintziras, "This Is How Heidi Montag and Spencer Pratt Lost Their $10 Million Net Worth," *TheThings*, updated August 11, 2022, https://www.thethings.com/this-is-how-heidi-montag-and-spencer-pratt-lost-their-10-million-net-worth-money/.

15. Lex Briscuso, "'The Hills' Alums Heidi Montag and Spencer Pratt's Net Worth is Lower Than You Think," *Life & Style*, November 17, 2022, https://www.lifeandstylemag.com/posts/heidi-montag-spencer-pratt-net-worth-how-much-money-they-have/.

16. Natalie Finn, "Gary Busey's Stuff Detailed for Bankruptcy Filing: VHS Tapes, Tepees and Tambourines," *E! News*, February 16, 2012, https://www.eonline.com/news/294957/gary-busey-s-stuff-detailed-for-bankruptcy-filing-vhs-tapes-tepees-and-tambourines.

17. AP, "Evander Holyfield's Mansion Under Foreclosure," *CNBC*, June 6, 2009, https://www.cnbc.com/id/24998497?&qsearchterm=evander%20holyfield.

18. Alan Hubbard, "Boxing: Holyfield's life goes under the hammer," *Independent*, October 14, 2012, https://www.independent.co.uk/sport/general/others/boxing-holyfield-s-life-goes-under-the-hammer-8210385.html.

19. Nick Vrchoticky, "The Reason Evander Holyfield Lost His Money," *The Grunge*, November 25, 2020, https://www.grunge.com/285364/the-reason-evander-holyfield-lost-his-money/.

20. "Lindsay Lohan's Financial Trouble: Where Did Her Money Go?," *HuffPost*, December 3, 2012, https://www.huffpost.com/entry/lindsay-lohan-financial-trouble_n_2234025.

21. Param Davies, "Falling From Grace: How Lindsay Lohan Lost Millions," *The Richest*, May 8, 202,1 https://www.therichest.com/rich-powerful/lindsay-lohan-lost-millions/.

22. "Lindsay Lohan – IRS Seizes Bank Accounts," *TMZ*, December 3, 2012, https://www.tmz.com/2012/12/03/lindsay-lohan-irs-bank-accounts-taxes/.

23. Mehera Bonner, "Lindsay Lohan's Net Worth Is a Roller-Coaster Ride, to Say the Least," *Yahoo! Life*, October 31, 2022, https://www.yahoo.com/lifestyle/lindsay-lohans-net-worth-roller-202800718.html.

24. Teejay Small, "Dennis Rodman's 2024 Net Worth Doesn't Reflect It, But He's The Most Fascinating Man on Earth," *Yahoo! Sports*, April 16, 2024, https://sports.yahoo.com/dennis-rodman-net-worth-doesn-215832609.html.

25. Jordan Greer, "How did Dennis Rodman lose his money? Peggy Ann Fulford stole millions from Hall of Famer, other athletes," *The Sporting News*, May 7, 2023, https://www.sportingnews.com/us/nba/news/dennis-rodman-peggy-ann-fulford-lose-stole-money-athletes/dsxoaidjt6gzcepsspvyrosn.

26. "Dennis Rodman must pay $500K in child support," *Associated Press,* December 7, 2012, https://apnews.com/article/f55076ce0ce942408fac0141e076c834.

27. Erin Griffin, "What Red Flags? Elizabeth Holmes Trial Exposes Investors' Carelessness," *The New York Times*, November 4, 2021, https://www.nytimes.com/2021/11/04/technology/theranos-elizabeth-holmes-investors-diligence.html.

28. Agustino Fontevecchia, "Forbes 400: Full List of America's Richest People," *Forbes*, September 29, 2014, https://www.forbes.com/sites/afontevecchia/2014/09/29/forbes-400-full-list-of-americas-richest-people/.

29. Robert Hart, "Elizabeth Holmes—Theranos Fraudster and Ex-Billionaire—Gets Two Years Cut Off From Prison Sentence," *Forbes*, July 11, 2023, https://www.forbes.com/sites/roberthart/2023/07/11/elizabeth-holmes-theranos-fraudster-and-ex-billionaire-quietly-cuts-two-years-off-prison-sentence/.

30. Roomy Khan, "Theranos' $9 Billion Evaporated: Stanford Expert Whose Questions Ignited The Unicorn's Trouble," *Forbes,* February 17, 2017, https://www.forbes.com/sites/roomykhan/2017/02/17/theranos-9-billion-evaporatedstanford-expert-whose-questions-ignited-the-unicorn-trouble/.

31. John Carreyrou, "Hot Startup Theranos Has Struggled With Its Blood-Test Technology," *The Wall Street Journal*, October 16, 2015, https://www.wsj.com/articles/theranos-has-struggled-with-blood-tests-1444881901.

32. Jaclyn Diaz, "Ramesh 'Sunny' Balwani is sentenced to nearly 13 years for his role in Theranos fraud," *NPR*, updated December 7, 2022, https://www.npr.org/2022/12/07/1141278121/theranos-sunny-balwani-sentencing-elizabeth-holmes.

Chapter 4

1. Tristan Hallman, "Dallas and Houston both have pension problems, but Houston is actually solving theirs," *The Dallas Morning News*, February 5, 2017, https://www.dallasnews.com/news/2017/02/05/dallas-and-houston-both-have-pension-problems-but-houston-is-actually-solving-theirs/.

2. "Client Behavior 101," Kemper Corporation, 1994.

3. "The Average Investor Is His Own Worst Enemy," *Forbes*, July 16, 2012, https://www.forbes.com/forbes/2010/0628/investment-guide-behaviorial-finance-odean-average-investor-own-enemy.html.

4. "ProShares UltraShort S&P 500, Advanced Charting," *Wall Street Journal*, https://www.wsj.com/market-data/quotes/mutualfund/SDS/advanced-chart.

5. "CFPB Study Details the Rapid Growth of 'Buy Now, Pay Later' Lending," *U.S. Consumer Financial Protection Bureau*, September 15, 2022, https://www.consumerfinance.gov/about-us/newsroom/cfpb-study-details-the-rapid-growth-of-buy-now-pay-later-lending/.

6. Moretti, Michael, "Laser Center Companies Develop US Market," *Journal of Refractive Surgery* 12, no. 4 (May 1996): 451–53. doi:10.3928/1081-597X-19960501-03.

7. Ryan Beene and Josh Saul, "Wind Turbines Taller Than the Statue of Liberty Are Falling Over," *Bloomberg*, January 23, 2023, https://www.bloomberg.com/news/articles/2023-01-23/wind-turbine-collapses-punctuate-green-power-growing-pains.

8. Wind Energy Technology Offices, "Statistics Show Bearing Problems Cause the Majority of Wind Turbine Gearbox Failures," *Office of Energy Efficiency & Renewable Energy*, https://www.energy.gov/eere/wind/articles/statistics-show-bearing-problems-cause-majority-wind-turbine-gearbox-failures.

Chapter 6

1. Thorsten Polleit, "100 Years Ago Today: The End of German Hyperinflation," *Mises Institute*, "Mises Daily," November 15, 2023, https://mises.org/mises-daily/100-years-ago-today-end-german-hyperinflation.

Slogans and Quotes

1. Richard Smitten, *Jesse Livermore: World's Greatest Stock Trader* (Hoboken, NJ: Wiley, 2002).
2. "CFPB Study Details the Rapid Growth of 'Buy Now, Pay Later' Lending," *U.S. Consumer Financial Protection Bureau*, September 15, 2022, https://www.consumerfinance.gov/about-us/newsroom/cfpb-study-details-the-rapid-growth-of-buy-now-pay-later-lending/.
3. Jonathan Clements, "Excuses, excuses: How losers save face," *South Coast Today*, updated January 12, 2011, https://www.southcoasttoday.com/story/business/2001/04/15/excuses-excuses-how-losers-save/50338880007/.

Chapter 7

1. Thomas J. Stanley and William D. Danko, *The Millionaire Next Door: The Surprising Secrets of America's Wealthy* (Lanham, MD: Taylor Trade Publishing, 2010).

Chapter 9

1. "Planning & Progress Study 2020," *Northwestern Mutual*, https://news.northwesternmutual.com/planning-and-progress-2020.

2. "Finding a Financial Advisor," *Peak Financial Planning*, May 16, 2024, https://www.thepeakfp.com/blog/finding-a-financial-advisor.

3. "7 Mistakes People Make When Choosing a Financial Advisor," *SmartAsset*, August 14, 2024, https://getadvisor.smartasset.com/bing-fa-mistakes/.

Chapter 10

1. "Stay invested: Don't risk missing the market's best days," *Fidelity Investments*, https://www.fidelity.com/bin-public/060_www_fidelity_com/documents/dont-miss-best-days.pdf.

Index

About the Author

After receiving his Bachelor of Science with a minor in engineering from the University of Texas at Austin in 1960, Dean McGowan began his journey in wealth management as a financial advisor and mutual and pension funds manager with Schneider, Bernet & Hickman, where he was the youngest partner in the firm throughout the early seventies. In 1974, Dean joined PaineWebber as assistant branch manager and went on to found the North Dallas branch of what later became UBS Financial Services. Before retiring from UBS in 2019, Dean would also found the McGowan Vehslage Goldberg Group (MVG Wealth Management).

Dean also proudly served three years on the New York Stock Exchange committee, during which he and other committee members rewrote the entire battery of three thousand questions for the

Series 7 (General Securities Representative) Exam, whose passing completion is required by brokers and other financial professionals in the U.S.

Volunteering in his community has remained equally important to Dean. For ten years he served as a board member of the Naveen Jindal School of Management in Richardson, Texas, where he mentored MBS students for eight years and served as a member of the school's financial department for four.

Dean has additionally been grateful to have had the privilege of serving as Treasurer, Chairman of the Elders, and Chairman of the Board for Community Christian Church in Richardson, as well as teaching Sunday school and serving in a lifestyle-coaching role for several years at Christ United Methodist Church's Project Hope in the city of Plano.